Two-for-One
FOUNDATION
PIECING
Reversible Quilts and More

Wendy Hill

C&T PUBLISHING

© 2001 Wendy Hill

Editor: Beate Marie Nellemann

Technical Editor: Karyn Hoyt and Joyce Lytle

Copy Editor: Stacy Chamness

Cover Designer: Kristen Yenche

Design Director/Book Designer: Kristen Yenche

Production Coordinator: Diane Pedersen

Illustrator: Richard Sheppard

Photographer: Steven Buckley, Photographic Reflections

Front cover quilt, *Sixteen Turkish Beauties*, was made by Debra Wruck

Production Assistant: Jeffery Carrillo

Published by C & T Publishing, Inc., P.O. Box 1456 Lafayette, California 94549

Library of Congress Cataloging-in-Publication Data
Hill, Wendy
  Two-for-one foundation piecing : reversible quilts and more / Wendy Hill.
     p. cm.
Includes bibliographical references and index.
  ISBN 1-57120-169-6 (trade pbk.)
  1. Patchwork—Patterns. 2. Quilting—Patterns. I. Title.
  TT835 .H4575 2001
  746.46'041—dc21
                          00-012993

Printed in Hong Kong
10 9 8 7 6 5 4 3 2 1

Dedication

For Reatha Marie Matthews and Allen Howard Stevens and April and Robert Hill

*If you followed your dreams
Where would they take you?*

Table of Contents

Acknowledgments

I followed a dream in writing this book, but I didn't take this path alone. C&T Publishing, my honorable partner, shared the vision with me. Thank you to everyone on my editorial team!

Students have explored the possibilities of reversible-foundation pieced quilts in my workshops the past several years. I thank all of them. Without you, I wouldn't have workshops to teach.

I am in debt to all the friends, who extended helping hands and listening ears, especially in the final months of putting the book together. Laura Clark, who spent her annual vacation time sewing and sewing and sewing, deserves an extra round of applause, as do Larraine Scouler and Debra Wruck, both of whom made beautiful projects for the book.

Thank you, Marta Woodward, for stepping out of your life as mother and wife for a few days and modeling the clothing in this book. A big thanks to Matteo Pierazzi for looking so cute on the baby quilt. The Hill Family is grateful for the Ramey Family for opening the doors to their guest suite whenever we drop into Nevada City, California.

To my husband, son, and extended family: there is life-after-the-book. Let's celebrate!

I am pleased to show off the work of several contributors, who took the "basic technique" and ran with it, making beautiful reversible quilted pieces. Please read about these people in the MEET THE CONTRIBUTORS section on page 92.

Don't stop reading yet. The following companies generously gave me fabric, patterns, or other products to make many of the projects and samples shown in this book. I hope they will be as pleased with the results as I am. Please refer to the RESOURCES section on page 93 for more information.

D'Leas Fabric & Button Studio

Fabric Collections & Cutting Corners

HOBBS Bonded Fibers®

Hoffman Fabrics California-International

Janome America, Inc

P&B Textiles

Schmetz Needles & Mega Sheen Thread

Sulky of America®

The Sewing Workshop

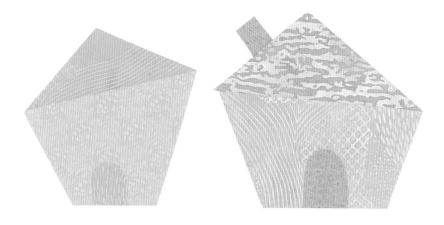

I followed a dream, or rather an idea, that came to me one early morning, in that mixed-up state of being half-awake and half-asleep. I imagined using foundation piecing to make reversible blocks for quilts and clothing. I bolted out of bed to try the idea. It worked. I immediately made a reversible Log Cabin quilt, something I have wanted to do for over twenty-five years.

If you can sew on a line, you too will be able to make reversible-foundation pieced blocks to use in quilts, clothing and more. With this technique, fabrics are pinned onto both sides of the foundation material. One stitching line sews through all the layers, simultaneously creating both sides of the block in one swoop.

Reversible-foundation pieced projects are fun to make and surprising to see. Like magic, the item is flipped over to reveal a different and second piece of work. Ask people who have used this technique and you'll find many reasons for getting hooked.

REASONS FOR GETTING HOOKED

TOPPERS: Some people, known as "toppers," love to design, plan, and make quilt tops, but get bogged down at the quilting stage. Reversible-foundation-pieced quilts are functionally quilted through the process of making the blocks. Many toppers have told me: "When you're done assembling the blocks, you're done!"

ECONOMY: Substitute a second set of fabrics instead of the backing fabric, combine it with only one batt or other foundation material. Add a wee-bit of extra time to pin both sides and you have the formula for two quilted items in one.

DURABILITY: Stitching through the batting results in close quilting. The finished project is very sturdy.

FLEXIBILITY: Reversible-foundation piecing allows you to work with two color schemes and create two different looks in the same quilted item:

▼ Make a garment for work and play; with a flick of the wrist the garment turns inside out, ready for the next activity.

▼ Sew a bed quilt for "him" and "her," and resolve the decorating controversy with a quick flip of the quilt.

▼ Create reversible wall hangings, table runners, and place mats; redecorate the house for the holidays, seasons, or for a whole new look—all without paint.

▼ Design two-sided quilted items with two color schemes; succumb to whimsy, mood, or indecision with a flip to the reverse side.

To get the most out of this book, take a look through all of the chapters first. Read about the technique in Chapter 1 but don't give up if it seems confusing. It is easier to do than to read about. Turn to Chapter 2 and teach yourself the basic technique with the step-by-step photographs and illustrations. Make just one Log Cabin practice block or put your practice to good use with a small nine-block wall hanging.

Choose from seven projects in Chapter 3. If you can't decide where to begin, plan to make them all! Chapter 4 introduces a GALLERY of inspiring samples to whet your appetite. Chapter 5, LOOK IT UP! provides a basic technique checklist and an alphabetical list of terms for quick reference. Words or phrases shown in color in the text can be found in this section.

Reversible-foundation piecing doesn't end with the last page of this book. Just about any foundation piecing pattern may be reverse pieced, so look at your collection of foundation-piecing patterns with a new "double vision." You'll be sewing double in no time.

FOUNDATION PIECING VERSUS REVERSIBLE-FOUNDATION PIECING

Foundation piecing is an old idea early quiltmakers used to sew scraps of fabric together; the paper or fabric foundation provided stability for all the bits of off-grain fabrics. Today foundation piecing is used to sew more than scrappy quilts. Foundation-piecing patterns use block designs with straight-seam sequences. All the seams must be straight lines and the pieces must go together in numerical order, with each new seam covering up the previous seam(s). The pattern lines are drawn onto the temporary or permanent foundation material. The generously cut fabrics are pinned on the unlined or plain side of the foundation, and then the whole thing is flipped over with the sewing done on the appropriate seam line. It is incredibly accurate, allowing people of all skill levels to sew very complex block patterns. The finished, pieced side of the foundation is the mirror image of the drawn, lined side of the block.

Reversible-foundation piecing is based on the same concepts as one-sided foundation piecing. Similarities include using the same source of straight-seam sequenced block patterns, sewing the pieces in numbered sequence on a marked line, and using generously cut pieces of fabric. Reversible-foundation piecing is just as easy, fast, and accurate as one-sided, but at the end of your sewing, you have a reversible, two-sided block.

A Few Important Differences

There are a few important differences with reversible-foundation piecing. The foundation material is permanently sandwiched in the block so temporary foundation materials, such as paper, cannot be used. Instead of planning for and using one color scheme, with reversible-foundation piecing you'll be putting together and organizing two different color schemes. One stitching line sews through all of the layers; both sides of the block are constructed at once. This also means the blocks are functionally quilted as you go; no additional, visible quilting is required. The finished pieced block is essentially two quilted patterns, both mirror images of each other.

Perhaps the biggest difference between one-sided and reversible, two-sided blocks is the final assembly into a "top." Normally blocks are sewn together into a top, which is then layered with batting and backing fabric, then quilted and bound. When reversible, two-sided blocks are sewn together, there are two quilt "tops" already QUILTED, but only one side is completely finished. The other side will have exposed seams or sashing strips which must be finished by hand or machine sewing.

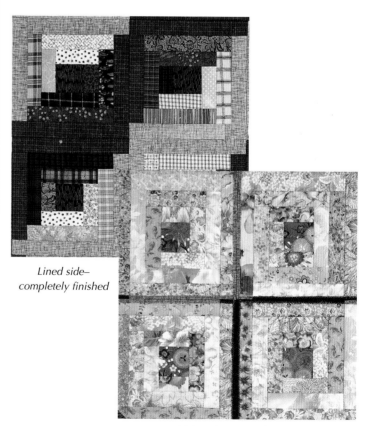

*Lined side—
completely finished*

*Plain side—exposed seams
must be covered up*

Although it might seem mind boggling at first to think and sew "double," the technique itself is easy to use with a little practice. There is a relaxing rhythm to following the steps. And there is really good news: once the reversible, two-sided blocks are put together, everything is done except the binding. When you're done, you're done!

GETTING THE BIG PICTURE

Since almost any foundation-pieced pattern may be made reversible, there is a wealth of patterns available in books and magazines. Finding uses for reversible blocks is easy: anything that can be turned inside-out or over is fair game for reversible-foundation piecing. Consider making quilts of all sorts and sizes, place mats, table runners, tote bags, name tags, coasters, and clothing of all kinds. You'll have two of everything you make.

Planning Ahead

Even if you don't normally do much planning with drawings, mock blocks, or fabric organization, it is highly recommended you try it when making reversible-foundation pieced projects. The truth is you are making two quilted items, with two color schemes but with an important difference. The two sides are mirror images and are not independent of each other. Moving or rotating block images on one side automatically moves or rotates the block images on the other side. A quilter's mind can only take so much confusion, and a little time spent in making plans will save your sanity, and spare you a date with the seam ripper.

Sanity Savers

SKETCH

A simple sketch of both sides of the block pattern, with notes, is often sufficient for simple color schemes or Repeat blocks.

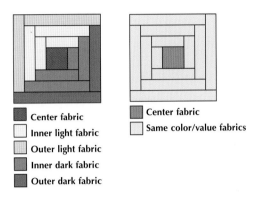

■ Center fabric
□ Inner light fabric
□ Outer light fabric
■ Inner dark fabric
■ Outer dark fabric

■ Center fabric
□ Same color/value fabrics

MOCK BLOCKS

Add snips of fabric to the sketches of both sides of the block pattern for a quick visual guide.

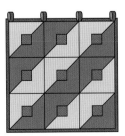

Lined side—mock block   *Plain side–mock block*

FULL SCALE DRAWING

More complicated block patterns or color schemes demand a drawing of both sides of the entire quilt.

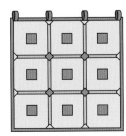

Lined side—full quilt   *Plain side—full quilt*

FABRIC ORGANIZATION

If you are comfortable with a heap of fabrics when sewing, make two or more separate heaps—made out of the two different color schemes. Other people like to make tidy stacks of fabrics; for reversible-foundation piecing, make separate piles of neatly stacked fabrics.

Several heaps of fabric

Neat stacks of fabric

Typical Supplies

Collecting fabric for a project becomes twice the fun with reversible-foundation piecing. This is your opportunity to make two distinct quilted items, so remember to plan the color scheme for each side independently. Much of the magic and fun of reversible-foundation-pieced items is in the surprise from one side to the other.

The foundation material is permanently sandwiched in the middle of the block and must withstand ironing. Match the foundation material to the final use of the finished project, taking into consideration weight, thickness, drape, loft, and so on. For example, wool batting might be the best choice for a warm bed quilt, while very thin cotton might be best for a jacket.

There are a variety of choices for foundation material in the following categories:

▼ Batting: cotton, cotton/polyester blend, wool, silk

▼ Woven Fabric: muslin, flannel, organdy, broadcloth, lightweight (non-fusible) interfacing

▼ Non-Woven Material: nylon stabilizer, lightweight (non-fusible) interfacing

A variety of other supplies are often used in reversible, foundation-pieced projects:

▼ Lightweight, non-woven fusible interfacing— to use with most battings

▼ Heat-activated transfer pen or pencil, such as Sulky brand, available in an assortment of colors from light to dark

▼ Template plastic or lightweight cardboard

▼ Favorite marking pen or pencil with a sharp point

▼ Graph paper or plain paper for making plans

▼ Rotary cutter/grid ruler/mat

▼ Walking foot

▼ Wooden dowel for hanging wall quilts

Foundation Blocks

This term is used to describe the foundation material after it has been prepared for sewing. Prewash most woven foundation materials. Prewash batting only as indicated by the instructions on the package; most non-woven materials do not need to be prewashed.

Most types of batting must be stabilized with fusible interfacing. The interfacing also provides a smooth surface for the foundation pattern seam lines. The exception is batting with a smooth "scrim" binder, which keeps the batting from stretching and is smooth enough to hold the marked seam lines.

Start with a master block: an accurate, scale drawing of the foundation-piecing pattern. Hand-trace the master block onto the foundation material or make multiple copies with a heat-activated transfer pen.

For peak efficiency, prepare all the foundation blocks at one time. For one-block projects, trim off the excess foundation material, leaving the desired seam allowance around the outside seam line. If the blocks will be joined together or with sashing, trim off the excess batting on the outside seam line to reduce bulk in the seams.

Block Construction

The principle of foundation piecing is to construct both sides of the block at the same time. The unstitched foundation block has a "lined side" and a "plain side." The lined side shows the seam lines of the foundation pattern. Flip over the foundation block; this side is blank. Work almost always begins on the lined side, but unlike one-sided foundation piecing, fabric is pinned right sides together on both sides of the foundation block.

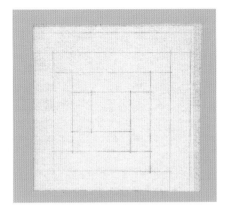

Foundation block–lined side

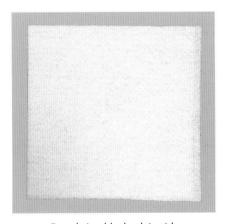

Foundation block–plain side

One stitched seam sews through all the layers at once, creating both sides of the block simultaneously and functionally quilting the block at the same time. As each piece is sewn to both sides, the seams are graded and ironed. There are four layers of fabric on top of each other in the seams. Grading the seams—trimming one seam narrower than the other—helps to reduce bulk. Step-by-step ironing is crucial for crisp, flat blocks with no pleats or tucks. This set of steps repeats until the block is finished. Photographs on next page.

Lined side—trimming seam allowance

Plain side—trimming seam allowance

The finished blocks are "squared-up", adding the seam allowance beyond the batting. For this technique use a $^3/_8$" seam allowance. I iron my seams open when connecting blocks. With the wider seam allowance, the ironed seams lie more flat. Use a grid ruler or a plastic see-through template to square up the blocks. Zigzag around the edges of the blocks, within the seam allowance. This keeps the edges together and the block flat. The blocks are ready for assembly.

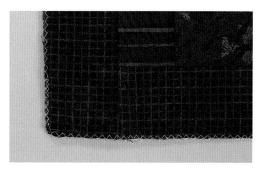

Zigzagged finished edges

Connecting the Blocks

When planning a foundation pieced reversible project, how the blocks will be joined is always an important and early consideration. There are two choices for connecting the blocks.

BLOCK-TO-BLOCK

One side of the blocks is sewn right sides together. Iron the seams open. Lightly whipstitch the seams—without going all the way through the layers—to keep them flat. Cover up the seams with bias strips, straight grain strips, or tubes. Blindstitch the seam coverings in place. Exploit the use of the seam coverings in the overall design, allowing them to blend in or to show off in sharp contrast. Since part of the block pattern is lost under the seam coverings, some patterns may not be suitable for block-to-block assembly.

Blending seam coverings

Contrasting seam coverings

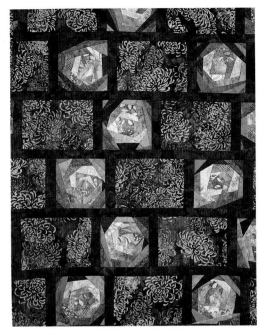
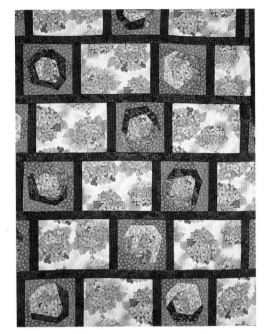

Narrow sashing

SASHING

Any reversible, two-sided blocks may be joined with sashing without losing any of the block patterns. Any width sashing may be used. Add additional foundation material to the sashing for consistent weight and loft. Very wide sashing may require additional quilting. Consider all sorts of fabrics for the sashing, including stripes, prints, or pieced strips.

Finishing Up

All projects with only one block, such as place mats, coasters, ornaments, name tags, one-block wall hangings and so on, are finished with the addition of binding. Other projects begin as a group of reverse-pieced blocks or strips, which must be sewn together. Borders may be added; remember to add additional foundation material. Quilting through the layers is always an option, but not required. Bind the outside edge with the usual single-fabric/double French-fold binding, or make an exciting two-fabric/double French-fold binding for your reversible project. Hang wall quilts with clamps or a dowel.

Two-fabric/Double French-fold binding

SUMMARY

If you can sew on a line, you'll now be able to make your favorite foundation-pieced projects reversible. Just about any foundation pattern works and the same basic steps apply to almost any project. It is easy, accurate, and fun, but if reading about it doesn't convince you, continue on to the next chapter. Here you will read and sew along with the step-by-step photographs and illustrations to guide you. Go ahead and make something reversible.

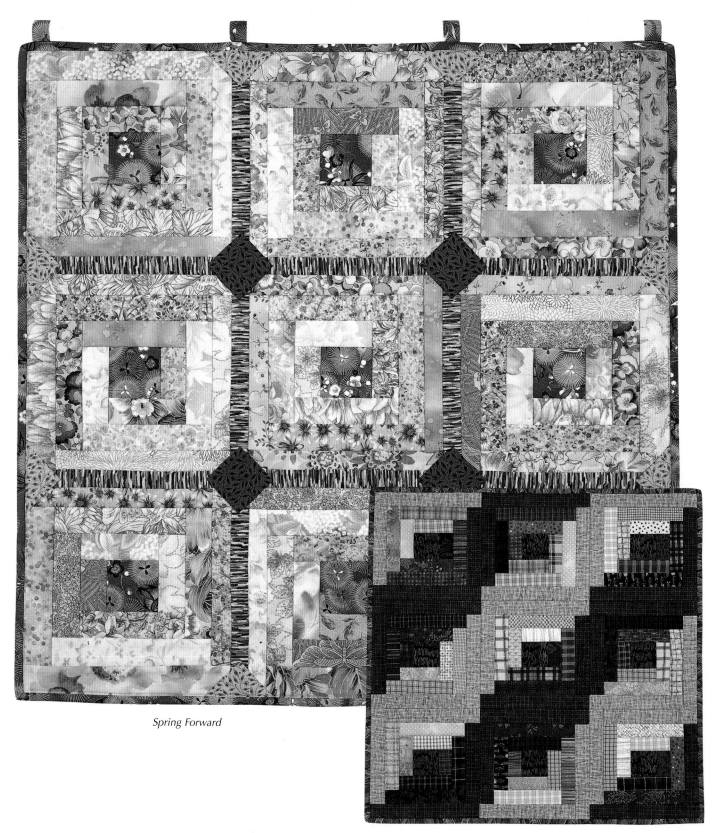

Spring Forward

Fall Back

LEARNING BY DOING

It is much easier to make a reversible-foundation-pieced block than to read about it. Of all the different kinds of foundation-pieced patterns, Log Cabin is probably the simplest to reverse piece. The basic steps are the same with any pattern, so once you understand the process with Log Cabin blocks, you'll be able to apply your knowledge to other projects. This chapter will take you through the process with step-by-step photographs and drawings. It is highly recommended you make at least one Log Cabin block by following along with each step.

Make your practice count and plan to use your Log Cabin practice blocks. Turn one Log Cabin block into a tiny wall hanging or a small table mat. Make a total of nine Log Cabin blocks for a small wall hanging. If you find you just love to make these blocks, turn to the project on page 35 and make a total of thirty-six blocks for a large wall hanging.

PRACTICE BLOCKS: DAYLIGHT SAVINGS TIME: FALL BACK/ SPRING FORWARD

Follow the color scheme shown for this Log Cabin quilt or plan your own color palette. The lined side, Fall Back, features warm fall colors with a traditional placement of fabrics to make the block half light and half dark. These Repeat blocks are rotated to make diagonal lines across the quilt top.

The plain side, Spring Forward, combines a large assortment of similar color and value floral fabrics. The randomly placed fabrics make the blocks appear the same. However, except for the center, the blocks are not identical. The result is a beautiful, luminous assortment of fabrics with no light/dark pattern to the block.

The two color schemes contrast with each other beautifully, and lend the quilt a seasonal feeling. But there is an ulterior motive behind the color scheme: simplicity. Remember, rotating or moving the Fall Back-side of the blocks also rotates and moves the image on the Spring Forward-side. Having all the same colors/values on one side eliminates the need to make detailed plans because rotating the image on this side doesn't change anything.

The blocks are sewn block-to-block, right sides together, from the Fall Back-side. The exposed seams are ironed open, whipstitched down, and covered up with tubes, squares-on-point, and half-square triangles. Think of this as an opportunity to exploit the visual impact of the design—but definitely not as a chore.

Supplies and Cutting Guide for Nine Log Cabin Block Wall Hanging

LINED SIDE —FALL COLORS

Center squares: $1/8$ yard one dark fabric—cut nine $3^1/4$" squares.

Inner light logs: $1/2$ yard total assorted fabrics—cut into $2^1/4$"-wide strips.

Outer light logs: $1/2$ yard one fabric—cut into $2^1/4$"-wide strips.

Inner dark logs: $1/2$ yard total assorted dark fabrics—cut into $2^1/4$"- wide strips.

Outer dark logs: $1/2$ yard one fabric—cut into $2^1/4$"-wide strips.

Binding and loops: $1/4$ yard one fabric—cut one rectangle $2^1/4$" by 10" and cut four 1"-wide strips.

PLAIN SIDE —SPRING COLORS

Center squares: $1/8$ yard one dark fabric—cut nine $3^1/4$" squares.

All logs: 2 yards assorted floral fabrics—cut into $2^{1}/_{4}$"-wide strips.

Squares-on-point: $^{1}/_{8}$ yard one dark fabric—cut four $2^{3}/_{4}$" squares.

Half-square triangles: $^{1}/_{8}$ yard one medium fabric—cut four $3^{3}/_{8}$" squares, then cut in half on the diagonal to make eight half-square triangles.

Tubes: $^{1}/_{4}$ yard medium one contrasting fabric—cut three strips 2" wide.

Binding and loops: $^{3}/_{8}$ yard one fabric—cut one rectangle $2^{1}/_{4}$" by 10" and cut four $1^{7}/_{8}$"-wide strips.

OTHER SUPPLIES

Cotton low-loft batting—cut nine 11" squares.

Non-woven, lightweight fusible interfacing: $1^{3}/_{4}$ yards—cut nine $10^{3}/_{4}$" squares.

Heat-activated transfer pen—any color except white

Template plastic or lightweight cardboard—cut one strip $1^{1}/_{4}$" by 13".

One sheet graph paper—at least 11" square

Favorite marking pencil or pen—with a sharp point

Rotary cutter/mat/grid ruler

Walking foot

Wooden dowel—$^{3}/_{4}$" in diameter by 31" long

Step-by-Step Directions:

Plan ahead with a sketch, drawing, or mock block.

Use the drawings and diagrams with each project to make your own plans. When designing your own projects, make similar kinds of plans to keep both sides straight.

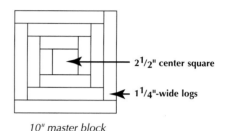

2$^{1}/_{2}$" center square
1$^{1}/_{4}$"-wide logs

10" master block

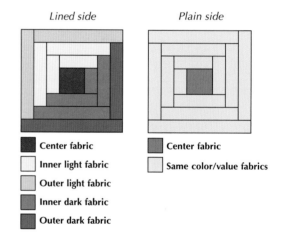

Lined side   Plain side

■ Center fabric
□ Inner light fabric
▨ Outer light fabric
▨ Inner dark fabric
■ Outer dark fabric

■ Center fabric
▨ Same color/value fabrics

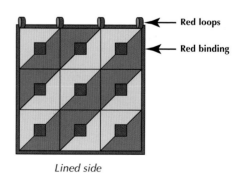

Red loops
Red binding

Lined side

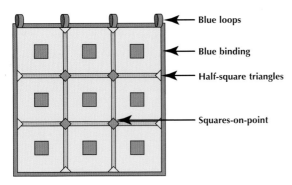

- ← Blue loops
- ← Blue binding
- ← Half-square triangles
- ← Squares-on-point

Plain side

Lined side—mock block

Plain side—mock block

Draft the Master Block

Use the given dimensions to draft the master block on graph paper. The master block is the source of all copies; make sure it is VERY accurate.

Prepare the Foundation Blocks

Gather the precut batting and interfacing, the master block, heat-activated transfer pen and grid ruler.

Ink the master block, following the instructions with the product. Test the pen on a scrap of paper. Press lightly and evenly, going over each line twice.

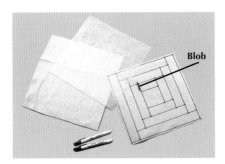

Blob

Finished inked master block

TIP

When making multiple copies, move the stack around to different areas of the ironing board. The ironing board cover can get very hot with this process.

Fuse the interfacing and transfer the master block in one step. Make a stack on the ironing board: batting, interfacing—bumpy side down, and master block—ink side down. Place and press the master block with the hot iron. Set the heat according to the instructions with the product. Do not "slide and glide" with the iron; this will smear the copy. Lift up a corner of the master block to see if the lines are dark enough—while still holding it in place. When the ink is fresh, the lines transfer more quickly than after several copies have been made.

Ironing the block

Lifting iron from the block

TIP

If the ink comes out in a "blob"; let it dry, then cover up the blob with masking tape.

Repeat this process to make the total number of foundation blocks needed.

Trim off the excess batting by cutting on the outside seam line, using a grid ruler for accuracy. This reduces bulk in the seams when the blocks are joined. When piecing the block, the last pieces of fabric will extend beyond the cut edge of the batting, forming the seam allowance.

Trimming the excesss batting

Prewash, precut, and organize the fabric.

CONSTRUCT THE BLOCKS

Pieces 1 and 2:

1. Start on the lined side of the foundation block. Pin-poke all four corners of Piece 1.

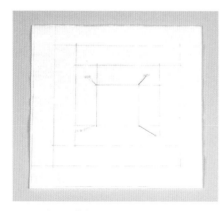

Pin-poking all four corners on the lined side

2. Flip the foundation block to the plain side. Position and pin Piece 1, plain side color scheme, over the pins, so there is an equal seam allowance all the way around. Pin at the sides.

Pin-poked corners on plain side

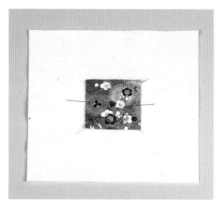

Position and pin the sides.

3. Flip the foundation block to the lined side. Position and pin Piece 1, lined side color scheme, over the pins, so there is an equal seam allowance all the way around. Pin at the bottom. Remove the pin-poke pins.

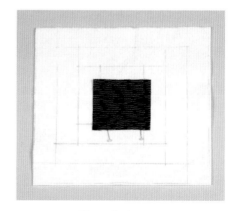

Pin at the bottom.

4. Continue on the lined side. Use the template to pin-poke the corners of the first seam line.

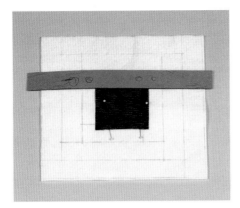

Lined side—pin-poke the first seam line.

5. Flip to the plain side. Cut a piece of fabric from an inner light strip, the same length as Piece 1. Position and pin Piece 2 right sides together with Piece 1, plain side color scheme. Use the pin-pokes as a guide. Fold back the seam allowance a scant $1/4$". Line up the folded edge with the spot where the pins come out of the fabric. Let the seam allowance fall into place. Pin at the edges of the fabric.

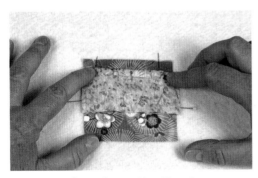

Plain side—position Piece 2.

6. Flip to the lined side. Position and pin Piece 2 right sides together with Piece 1, lined side color scheme. Use the pin-pokes as a guide. Fold back the seam allowance a scant $1/4$". Line up the folded edge with the spot where the pins go into the fabric. Let the seam allowance fall into place. Pin about an inch from the edges of the log, to avoid pins being on top of each other front and back. Remove the pin-poke pins. Check to make sure the fabrics are "behaving"—lying

smooth and flat. If not, do it over, pinning through just the top layer of the foundation block.

Lined side—position and pin Piece 2.

7. Continue on the lined side. Use the template to mark the seam line with your favorite marking pen or pencil.

Lined side—marking the seam line, using template

8. Using a normal stitch length and a walking foot, stitch along the marked line, beginning and ending 1-2 stitches beyond the actual seam line.

Lined side—sewing Piece 1 and 2

9. Check placement of fabrics on both sides. Finger press Piece 2 into position—it should extend at least ¼" beyond the seam line above. If not, rip out the stitches and do it over.

Lined side—check placement.

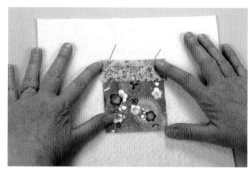

Plain side—check placement.

10. Grade the seam allowances on both sides. To do this, trim one fabric narrower than the other. If the lighter fabric is on top, trim the darker fabric narrower, so the lighter fabric extends beyond the darker fabric.

Lined side—trimming seam allowance

Plain side—trimming seam allowance

11. Iron-up Piece 2, first one side of the block, and then the other.

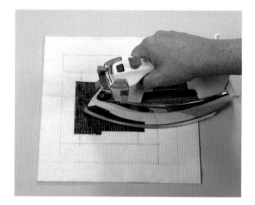

Lined side—iron-up.

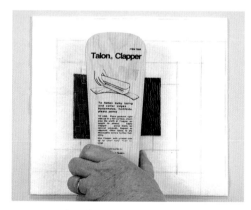

Using the Clapper—see pages 83 and 87.

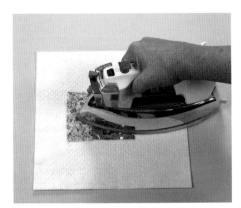

Plain side—iron-up

Using the Clapper—see pages 83 and 87.

Continue with remaining Pieces 3-13.

12. Flip to the lined side. Use the template to mark the seam line. Pin-poke the ends of the next seam line.

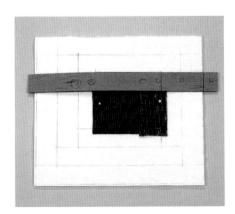

Lined side—pin-poke seam line.

13. Flip to the plain side. Position and pin Piece 3 (plain side color scheme) right sides together along seam line. Fold back a scant $^1/_4$", line up with the spot where the pins come out of the fabric, let the seam allowance fall into place, and pin at the sides.

Plain side—pin-poking

Plain side—pinning Piece 3

Flip to the lined side. Position and pin Piece 3, lined side color schemes right sides together, along the seam line. Fold back a scant $^1/_4$", line up with the spot where the pins go into the fabric, let the seam allowance fall into place, and pin about 1" from the sides. Remove the pin-poke pins. Photograph next page.

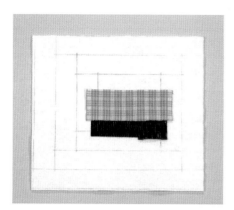

Lined side—Piece 3

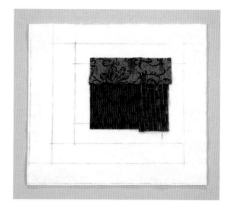

Lined side—Piece 3 finished and ironed-up

Continue on lined side. Use the template to mark the seam line with marking pen or pencil. Check to make sure the fabrics are "behaving."

Lined side—marking the seam line

Plain side—Piece 3 finished and ironed-up

Continue on the lined side. Stitch along the marked seam line, beginning and ending 1-2 stitches beyond the actual seam line.

14. Check the fabric placement by finger pressing Piece 3 in place to make sure it extends at least $1/4$" beyond the seam line above. If not, rip out the stitches, and do it over. Grade the seam allowance on both sides. Iron-up each piece into place, first one side of the block, and then the other.

Repeat the Steps 12 to 14 with Pieces 4-13 to finish the block. Below is a summary of the steps:

Lined side: Pin-poke the ends of the seam line.

Plain side: Pin the "next piece" into place.

Lined side: Pin the same "next piece" into place.

Lined side: Use the template to mark seam line.

Lined side: Stitch seam line.

Both sides: Check the fabric placement; grade the seams; iron-up the pieces.

Lined side—finished Pieces 1-6

Plain side—finished Pieces 1-6

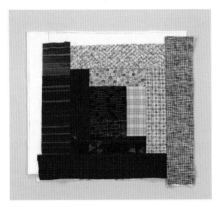

Lined side—almost finished block

Plain side—almost finished block

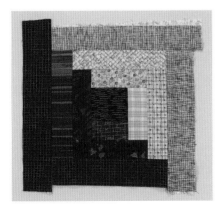

Lined side—finished block

Plain side—finished block

SQUARING-UP THE BLOCKS

Pin-poke the corners of the batting.

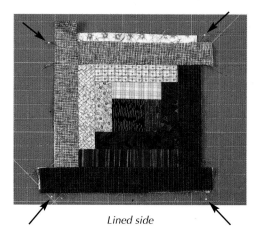

Lined side

Use a square grid ruler to add the $3/8$" seam allowance beyond the pins along the top and right side—for right-handed people. Line up the grid ruler lines with the seam lines for accuracy. Remove the pins.

Cut off the excess fabric.

Lined side—trimming first two sides

Turn the block around. Place the grid ruler on the trimmed edges at the $10^3/4$" line—10" block plus $3/8$" seam allowance on each side. Cut off the excess fabric.

Lined side—trimming sides

Pin around the edge making sure the fabric is flat.

Lined side—pinning outside strips

Zigzag around the outside edges using a narrow open setting.

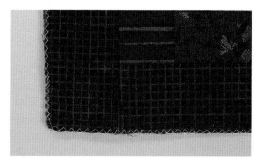

Lined side—finishing the edges with zigzagging

AUDITION THE BLOCKS

Lay out the blocks, with the fall color side up. Rotate the blocks to make diagonal lines.

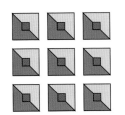
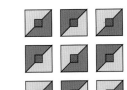

Fall color—or lined side up   *Rotated blocks*

To check out the spring color side, overlap and pin the edges of the blocks together in each row from the plain side. Flip the entire row over. It won't work to flip over individual blocks; remember the opposite side is the mirror image.

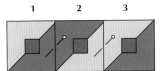
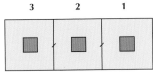

Lined side up, pinned at seams   *Flipped to plain side*

Move blocks around until you are satisfied.

ASSEMBLE BLOCK-TO-BLOCK

Start with the fall color side facing up. Sew the blocks right sides together with a $3/8$" seam allowance. Sew the blocks into rows, ironing the seams open. Sew the rows into a quilt panel, ironing the seams open.

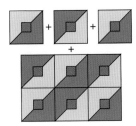

Sewing blocks together

Lightly whipstitch the seams down, just catching the fabric and using loose stitches.

Whipstitched blocks

COVER UP THE SEAMS

To make the tubes: sew the strips wrong sides together with a $1/4$" seam allowance. Iron the tubes flat, centering the seam down the middle of the tube. Cut twelve tubes, each 10" long.

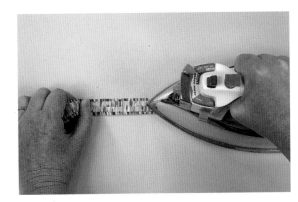

Ironing the tube

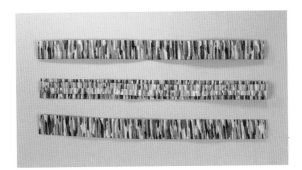

Finished tubes

Center the tubes over the seams following the diagram. Blindstitch in place.

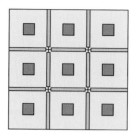

Seams covered with tubes

Placing the tubes on the plain side

Prepare the four squares and eight half-square triangles. Fold under the edges of the squares ¹/₄" on all sides. Finger-press or iron. Fold under the two right angle sides of the half-square triangles ¹/₄" as shown below.

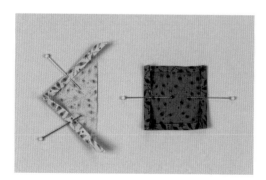

Preparing the squares and half-square triangles

Position the squares "on-point" at the intersections of the four blocks, centering the points in the center of the tubes. Blindstitch in place. Position the half-square triangles along the four sides of the quilt following the diagram. Center the points in the center of the tubes. Blindstitch in place.

Blindstitched squares and half-square triangles

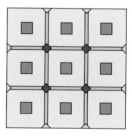

Positioned squares "on-point" and half-square triangles

LOOPS

Make a total of 4 two-fabric loops:

1. Pin and sew the two loop fabrics right sides together lengthwise. Use a ¹/₄" seam allowance. Iron the seams open.

The two loop fabrics sewn together

2. Cut a total of four pieces, each 4" x 2".

Cutting the loops

3. Fold lengthwise, right sides together, and sew with a $\frac{1}{4}$" seam allowance to form the tube.

4. Finger-press the seam open.

5. Turn right side out.

6. Iron each loop flat, centering the seam down the center of the loop.

Four steps making the loop

7. Fold the loop in half—seam inside—and whipstitch the raw edges together. Iron lightly to flatten the loop out.

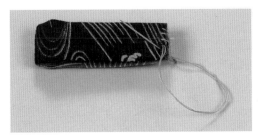

Whipped loop

8. Position the loops right sides (lined side) down on the quilt. The loops will be sandwiched in the seam between the quilt top and the binding. Instead of pinning, use a piece of masking tape to reduce bulk.

Positioning the loop

TWO-FABRIC/DOUBLE FRENCH-FOLD BINDING

1. Gather the precut binding strips. Starting with the 1" strips, miter the ends and sew the strips right sides together. Iron the seams open. Repeat with the $1\frac{7}{8}$" strips.

2. Sew the two long strips, right sides together, along one long edge, with a $\frac{1}{4}$" seam allowance. It is essential to iron the seam open.

Binding sewn together

3. Fold the binding in half and LIGHTLY iron or finger-press.

Lightly ironed, folded binding

4. Leave a 6" tail at the beginning. Use a $3/8$" seam allowance. Pin and sew the binding—narrow fabric down—right sides to the quilt, stopping $3/8$" from the first corner. Miter at the corner. Continue sewing corner to corner in this manner, stopping about 7" from the starting point. Miter and sew the ends right sides together, and finish sewing the binding to the quilt.

Sewing the binding to the quilt on the lined side

5. Open out the binding along the top edge. Push up the loops and finger-press to flatten them. Machine stitch—with matching thread—just below the seam line, between the two fabrics. This holds and strengthens the loops.

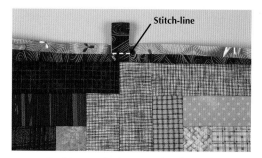

Stitch-line

Pushing up the loop on the plain side

6. Fold the binding over to the other side. The two different fabrics should "split" right at the seam line, resulting in one fabric on either side of the quilt. Blindstitch the binding in place, mitering at the corners.

Holding the binding from the lined side

Folding the binding

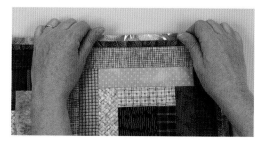

Finishing the binding on the plain side

SUMMARY

Turn to the Gallery, page 62, to find out what other people have accomplished with the same instructions you just followed. You might be surprised! You'll certainly be motivated to make your own reversible projects. Turn to the next chapter to start your own masterpiece.

Projects

S even exciting projects are presented here, with tips and ideas for additional applications. The projects model the use of strip-pieced patterns, Log Cabin blocks, Repeat blocks, Representational blocks, Crazy quilt blocks, and Fan type blocks. Each project opens a door into an imaginary room filled with more ideas for that kind of block. Step into the room, or go on down the hallway to the next door; it's up to you.

The basic technique—plus a few variations—are the same for all of the projects. In order to keep the directions straightforward and non-repetitious, key words in the directions— printed in purple—refer the reader to Chapter 5, Look It Up! With experience gained using reversible-foundation piecing, you'll know what these terms and phrases mean without having to look them up.

REVERSIBLE FLYING GEESE

62½" x 78"
Larraine Scouler

All sorts of patterns may be reverse-foundation pieced in strips, including wild goose chase, parallel strips, small and large triangles, equilateral triangles, braids and so on.

Connect the reverse pieced strips with sashing strips to make a panel the size needed for your project. In this case, Larraine designed a bed size quilt using two sizes of Flying Geese units; this eliminates the need to line up the geese on either side of the sashing strips and adds visual interest without going to any extra trouble. See pages 68, 74, and 76 for other examples of strip-pieced patterns.

Color Scheme

Larraine used a scrappy assortment of reds and yellows for one side of her quilt and bright primary colors and fussy (individually) cut animal prints for the other side. This would make a good quilt for an older child, one who might want to grow up a bit with the solid color side but who is still young enough to want to cuddle up with animal friends.

Lined side—animal prints

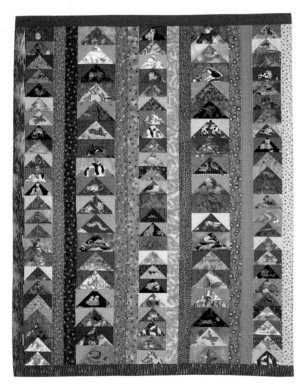

Lined side with animal prints

Plain side with warm reds and yellows

◀ *Reversible Flying Geese. Home of Sandra Bruce and Gary Pierazzi*

Fabric Selection Tip

At first glance, it may seem as though only true reds and yellows were used for the warm color side of the quilt. A closer look reveals the wide variety of reds and yellows in each group.

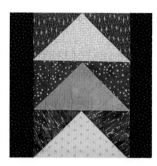

Plain side—warm reds and yellows

Imagine a color wheel. Larraine not only chose fabrics in all shades of red—fire engine red, brick red, rust red, and fuchsia—she knocked on the colors next door to use red-violets and red-oranges of all sorts. The same is true for the yellows. Larraine used all types of yellows—lemon yellow, mustard yellow, canary yellow, and Easter egg yellow. She went next door to use yellow-oranges and hints of dull yellow-greens. When using monochromatic color schemes, one color family, com-bining a variety of values is the most important thing to make the color scheme work.

Supply List

FABRICS FOR THE LINED SIDE: ANIMAL PRINTS WITH PRIMARY COLORS

Animal/feature print: $2\frac{1}{8}$ yards total to speed cut or collect enough to individually cut—seventy-two large and thirty-six small animals

Bright prints and solids to contrast: $2\frac{1}{8}$ yards total

Sashing: twelve bright fabrics—each $\frac{1}{4}$ yard

FABRICS FOR THE PLAIN SIDE WITH WARM REDS AND YELLOWS

Red prints: $2\frac{1}{4}$ yards total

Yellow prints: $2\frac{1}{8}$ yards total

Sashing: $2\frac{1}{8}$ yards one fabric

Seam covering strips: $\frac{3}{8}$ yard

OTHER SUPPLIES

Batting: 70" by 80" minimum

Non-woven, lightweight fusible interfacing: $4\frac{1}{2}$ yards

Binding: $\frac{3}{4}$ yard

Favorite marking pen or pencil with a sharp point

Template plastic

Rotary cutter/mat/long grid ruler

Walking foot

Preparation Instructions

PLAN AHEAD

Get ready to sew by making a sketch or mock strips showing fabric placement for both sides. Refer to the graph drawings for guidance.

FOUNDATION STRIPS

Cut three pieces of batting and interfacing, each 13" by 80". Cut two pieces each of batting and interfacing, 15" by 80".

Carefully fuse the interfacing to the batting. Whipstitch around the edges of the interfacing to keep it from coming loose with handling during sewing.

Draw the grid onto the prepared foundation strip. Using the long ruler and a marking pen, draw a line down the center of the full length of the strip. Using the grid ruler as a T-square, measure and draw cross lines at right angles to the center line: 3" apart for the small geese—13"-wide foundation strips, and 4" apart for the large geese—15"-wide foundation strips. You should have twenty-six spaces for the small geese and twenty for the large geese.

For the small geese, draw a parallel line 3" from each side of the center line and another line 2³/₄" beyond that line on each side.

For the large geese draw a parallel line 4" from each side of the center line and another line 2³/₄" beyond that line on each side.

Draw the diagonal lines for each of the geese on all the foundation strips.

Trim off excess batting on the outside seam line; use a grid ruler for accuracy. The small geese foundation strips should be 11¹/₂" wide by 78" long. The large geese foundation strips should be 13¹/₂" wide by 78" long.

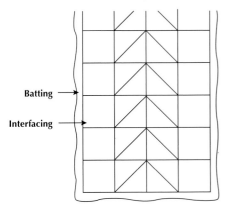

Foundation strip

TEMPLATES

Draw and cut one template for the small Flying Geese triangle, and one for the large Flying Geese triangle; finished size, no seam allowance added. Using permanent pen, draw a vertical line through the apex of both triangles.

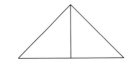

Template, 3" x 6"

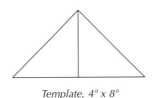

Template, 4" x 8"

Precutting Guide

LINED SIDE/ANIMAL PRINTS

If you decide to cut the animals individually as Larraine did, use the templates as a guide to cut thirty-six large animals and seventy-two small animals. Leave a generous ¹/₂" around the template when cutting out the animals.

USING ONE ANIMAL PRINT

Cut eighteen 8¹/₂" squares, cut again across both diagonals, to make a total of seventy-two quarter-square triangles.

Cut nine 10¹/₂" squares, cut again across both diagonals, to make a total of thirty-six quarter-square triangles.

LINED SIDE/BRIGHT PRINTS AND SOLIDS

Cut seventy-two 4¹/₂" squares, cut again once on the diagonal to make 144 half-square triangles.

Cut thirty-six 5¹/₂" squares, cut again once on the diagonal to

make seventy-two half-square triangles.

PLAIN SIDE/REDS AND YELLOWS

Red fabrics

Cut eighteen 8¹/₂" squares; cut again across both diagonals, to make a total of seventy-two quarter-square triangles.

Cut thirty-six 5¹/₂" squares; cut again once on the diagonal to make seventy-two half-square triangles.

Yellow fabrics

Cut nine 10¹/₂" squares; cut again across both diagonals to make a total of thirty-six quarter-square triangles.

Cut seventy-two 4¹/₂" squares; cut again once on the diagonal to make 144 half-square triangles.

SASHINGS

Lined side —Animal/bright prints

Cut two strips, each 4" wide, from each of twelve bright prints. Square up the ends and sew the short ends of matching pairs together, end to end, with a ³/₈" seam allowance. Iron the seams open. Cut each strip to 74", centering the seam in the center, 37" from each end.

Plain side—reds and yellows

Cut twelve strips, each 4" wide by the length of the fabric, parallel to the selvage, about 74".

Seam covering strips

Cut eight 1¹/₂" wide strips.

Directions

STRIP ASSEMBLY

Start with the lined side of the marked $11\frac{1}{2}$"-wide prepared foundation strip. Leave one space at the bottom of the strip and begin the strip assembly in second space up. Pin-poke the three corners of the triangle.

Flip to the plain side. Position and pin Piece 1, red fabric.

Flip to the lined side. Position and pin Piece 1, animal print.

Use the template to pin-poke the seam line on the left.

Flip to the plain side. Position and pin Piece 2, yellow fabric.

Flip to the lined side. Position and pin Piece 2, bright print or solid fabric.

Use the template to mark the seam line. Sew through all the layers. Check placement. Grade the seams. Iron-up Piece 2 on both sides.

Starting on the lined side, use the template to pin-poke the seam line on the right.

Flip to the plain side. Position and pin Piece 3, yellow fabric.

Flip to the lined side. Position and pin Piece 3, bright print or solid fabric.

Use the template to mark the seam line. Sew through all the layers.

Check placement. Grade the seams. Iron-up Piece 3 on both sides.

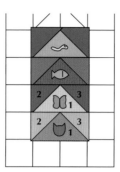

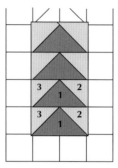

NOTE:

For clarity, the numbering starts over with each "goose"—set of three triangles.

Use the template to pin-poke the horizontal seam line.

Flip to the plain side. Position and pin Piece 1, red fabric.

Flip to the lined side. Position and pin Piece 1, animal print.

Use the template to mark the seam line. Sew through all the layers. Check placement. Grade the seams. Iron-up Piece 1 on both sides.

Repeat this until twenty-four Flying Geese have been pieced. There will be a space left over on the top and bottom of the strip for the sashing.

Repeat all steps to complete the two remaining $11\frac{1}{2}$"-wide foundation strips.

Repeat all steps for the $13\frac{1}{2}$"-wide foundation strips. There will be a total of eighteen Flying Geese, with a space left over on the top and bottom of each strip. Use these fabrics:

Lined side, Piece 1, animal print

Plain side, Piece 1, yellow fabric

Lined side, Piece 2 and 3, print or solid fabric

Plain side, Piece 2 and 3, red fabric

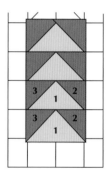

SASHING

1. The pieced part of the strips should measure $72\frac{1}{2}$" including the seam allowances. There will be extra batting at each end. Cut down all the sashing strips to the same measurement as the pieced part of the strips, $72\frac{1}{2}$" or your measurement.

2. Using the Flying Geese edge points as a guide, mark a $\frac{1}{4}$" seam allowance outside this line. Position the Side 1 sashing fabric with the raw edge on the marked line, pin and sew $\frac{1}{4}$" from the marked line. Check placement.

3. Flip to plain side. Mark a $\frac{1}{4}$" seam allowance outside the stitching line. Position the Side 2 sashing fabric with the raw edge on the marked line and pin.

4. Flip to the lined side. Stitch along the first seam line again. Check placement of the Side 2 border.

5. Grade both seam allowances. Iron-up the sashing on both sides.

6. Repeat Steps 2-5 to sew the sashing to the other side of the pieced Flying Geese strip.

7. Repeat Steps 2-6 for the remaining four foundation-pieced strips.

8. Square-up strips, allowing $\frac{3}{8}$" seam allowance on long edges. Do NOT trim short edges yet.

The small geese strips will be $12\frac{1}{4}$" wide total and the large geese strips will be $14\frac{1}{4}$" wide total.

9. Use bobbin thread to match the sashing fabric on the plain side and needle thread to match the sashing fabrics on the lined side. From the lined side, sew a line of topstitching on each sashing strip (through all the layers) $\frac{1}{4}$" away from the join with the Flying Geese panel. Repeat to topstitch both sides of sashing on each pieced strip changing thread colors as needed.

Quilt Assembly

1. Join the pieced strips, lined side, and right sides together, using a $\frac{3}{8}$" seam allowance. Iron the seams open, plain side.

2. Whipstitch the seams down or machine-baste. Basting will be removed later.

3. Connect the edges of the batting along the long outside edges with a loose whipstitch. The binding will later cover this.

4. Prepare the seam covering strips. Fold and press $\frac{3}{8}$" seam allowance under on both sides or use a bias tool to make a $\frac{3}{4}$"-wide strip.

5. Position the strips over the seams and pin or baste. Machine stitch through all of the layers, using a bobbin thread to match the sashing strips on the other side and a needle thread to match the strips. Remove the machine basting, if used.

6. Add the sashing to the top and bottom of the quilt using the same procedure in the sashing directions.

7. Use a single-fabric/double French-fold binding to finish the outside edges. Now, cuddle up under your new reversible quilt.

Fall Back—lined side

Spring Forward—plain side

DAYLIGHT SAVINGS TIME: FALL BACK/SPRING FORWARD

61" x 61"
Finished Block Size: 10"
Wendy Hill

It is easy to sing the praises of the humble Log Cabin block. With roots deep in quilting history, quilters are still using this block worldwide in both traditional and innovative ways. This is an easy block for beginner reversible-foundation piecers, because it requires only one template and oversized strips of fabric. See pages 67, 70, 71, and 78 for examples of more applications with Log Cabin blocks.

Color Scheme

The two color schemes make this Log Cabin quilt even easier. All of the blocks are constructed the same way, with very little planning ahead required. The fall color side of the blocks may be rotated to form the "barn raising" configuration without changing the overall image on the spring color side of the block.

FALL COLORS

Put together an assortment of folk prints, plaids, and hand-dyed cottons in warm reds and browns in high contrasting light and dark fabrics. For the light fabrics think warm beige and gold, pinkish reds, light teal, light red; for the dark fabrics think brick reds, dark teal or blue, rusty warm browns, and dark gold.

Detail from fall side–lined side

SPRING COLORS

Look for fabrics with similar colors and values in large and small floral prints and abstract designs. Choose color combinations with primarily pinks, yellows, yellow-oranges, yellow-greens, and lavenders, all with limited amounts of blues.

Detail from spring side–plain side

Fabric Selection Tip

Go into the fabric store with your "blinders" on. The shop will assault you with an abundance of beautiful fabrics, but you are looking for just the right ones to make up your large, scrappy assortment. Before you walk into the shop, review your notes about what kinds of fabric you are looking for. Pile up and consider all sorts of bolts of fabric without regard to whether they are folk prints, hand-dyeds, or abstract. If they seem to meet the color, value, and visual texture requirements, give the fabric a chance. Only after accumulating a big stack of bolts, eliminate the fabrics that don't "go" with the group. Always offer to help return bolts of fabric to the shelves to maintain a good relationship with the shop.

I used fifty-eight fabrics for the Fall Back side (lined side) of the quilt and thirty fabrics for the Spring Forward side (plain side). An equal number of bolts of fabric were rejected. The "thinking" for scrappy quilts is done when you leave the store with your fabrics. At home combine your fabrics randomly. You already know they will all work together across the quilt top just the way they did on the floor in the fabric shop.

Supply List

LINED SIDE—FALL COLORS

Center squares: $1/3$ yard one dark fabric—cut thirty-six $3^1/4$" squares.

Inner light fabrics: $1^1/2$ yards total assorted fabrics—cut into $2^1/4$"-wide strips.

Outer light fabrics: $1^1/2$ yards one fabric—cut into $2^1/4$"-wide strips.

Inner dark fabrics: $1^1/2$ yards total assorted dark fabrics—cut into $2^1/4$"-wide strips.

Outer dark fabrics: $1^1/2$ yards one fabric—cut into $2^1/4$"-wide strips.

Loops: $1/8$ yard one fabric—cut one strip $2^1/4$" by 18".

Binding: $1/4$ yard one fabric—cut seven, 1"-wide strips.

PLAIN SIDE—SPRING COLORS

Center squares: $1/3$ yard one dark fabric—cut thirty-six $3^1/4$" squares.

All logs: $5^1/2$ yards assorted floral fabrics—cut into $2^1/4$"-wide strips.

Squares on point: $1/8$ yard one dark fabric—cut thirteen $2^3/4$" squares.

Half-square triangles: $1/8$ yard one medium fabric—cut four $3^3/8$" squares; then cut in half on the diagonal to make eight half-square triangles.

Tubes: 1 yard one medium contrasting fabric—cut into $2^1/4$"-wide strips.

Loops: $1/8$ yard one fabric—cut one strip $2^1/4$" by 18".

Binding: $1/2$ yard one fabric—cut seven $1^7/8$"-wide strips.

OTHER SUPPLIES

Batting: cut thirty-six 11" squares.

Non-woven, lightweight fusible interfacing: six yards—cut thirty-six $10^3/4$" squares.

Heat-activated transfer pen—any color except white

Template plastic or lightweight cardboard—cut one strip $1^1/4$" by 13".

Favorite marking pen or pencil with a sharp point

One sheet graph paper—at least 11" square

Rotary cutter/mat/grid ruler

Walking foot

Wooden dowel for hanging — one $3/4$" diameter by 61" long

TIP

When prewashing a large assortment of fabrics, each under a $1/2$ yard in length, overlap the cut edges of similarly colored fabrics and zigzag together. Now you may wash a large piece of fabric without the fabric getting tangled around the agitator. Pampering your fabric early on will actually save you time later—and your fabrics will love you for it.

Directions

1. Plan ahead for your quilt with a sketch or mock blocks showing fabric placement for both sides. Refer to the drawings for guidance.

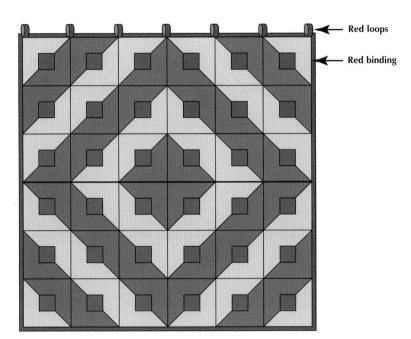

Red loops ←
Red binding ←

Fall Back—lined side

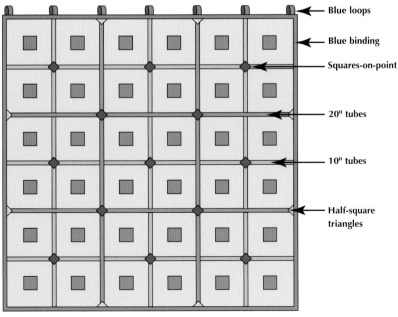

Blue loops ←
Blue binding ←
Squares-on-point ←
20" tubes ←
10" tubes ←
Half-square triangles ←

Spring Forward—plain side

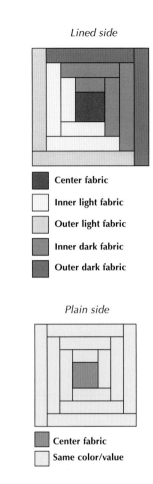

Lined side

- ■ **Center fabric**
- □ **Inner light fabric**
- ▨ **Outer light fabric**
- ▩ **Inner dark fabric**
- ■ **Outer dark fabric**

Plain side

- ▨ **Center fabric**
- □ **Same color/value**

Draft a master block using the graph paper.

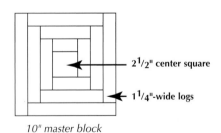

2¹/₂" center square ←
1¹/₄"-wide logs ←

10" master block

2. Prepare thirty-six foundation blocks using batting and fusible interfacing. Trim off the excess batting on the outside seam line; use a grid ruler for accuracy.

3. Prewash, precut, and organize the fabrics.

4. Use the basic technique to construct thirty-six blocks.

5. Square up the blocks with a $^3/_8$" seam allowance, $10^3/_4$" total. Zigzag the edges.

6. Lay out the blocks showing the fall color side. Rotate the blocks to make a Barn Raising pattern. Move blocks around until you are satisfied. To check the other side, overlap and pin the side edges of the blocks together into rows, and flip the whole row over. Before sewing, the fall color side should be facing up.

7. Assemble the quilt using the block-to-block method, with fall colors (lined side) sewn right sides together. Sew blocks into rows and the rows into a quilt top, using a $^3/_8$" seam allowance. Iron the seams open; whipstitch the seams down.

8. Make the tube seam coverings—thirty-six $^3/_4$" by 10" tubes and twelve $^3/_4$" by 20" tubes. Refer to the Spring Forward illustration on page 37 for placement. Blindstitch the 10" tubes in place first. See detail this page.

Blindstitch the 20" tubes in place, covering up the ends of the tube.

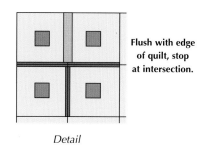

Flush with edge of quilt, stop at intersection.

Detail

PREPARE THE SQUARES AND HALF-SQUARE TRIANGLES

9. Fold over all four edges of the squares $^1/_4$", finger-press or pin and iron.

Fold over the two right angle sides of the half-square triangles $^1/_4$", finger-press or pin and iron.

10. Refer to page 37 and to detail below for placement. Position the squares and half-square triangles "on-point", so the points line up in the center of the tubes. Pin and blindstitch in place.

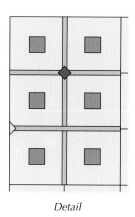

Detail

PREPARE THE LOOPS

11. Make seven, two-fabric loops, $^3/_4$" wide, using your dowel size to calculate the length.

12. Position and pin or tape the fall color side of the loops right side together with the fall color side of the quilt. Place one loop about 1" from the corners and one loop at each block seam. The loops will be sandwiched in the seam between the quilt top and the binding.

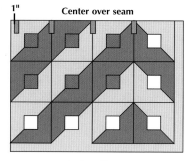

1"   **Center over seam**

Detail

Make the Two Fabric/Double French Fold Binding

13. Make the binding —two-fabric/double French fold. Position and pin the side with the narrow fabric right sides to the fall color side of the quilt. Use a $3/8$" seam allowance, miter at each corner, miter the ends together, and finish the seam.

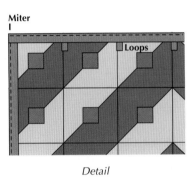

Detail

14. Open out the binding along the top edge. Push up the loops and finger-press to flatten them out a bit. Machine stitch the loop to the binding (with matching thread) just below the seam line between the two fabrics. This strengthens and holds the loops in place.

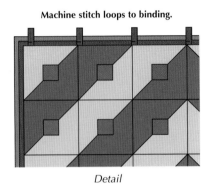

Machine stitch loops to binding.

Detail

15. Fold the binding over at the seam line between the two fabrics. Hand-sew the binding in place, mitering at the corners. Hang the quilt and enjoy!

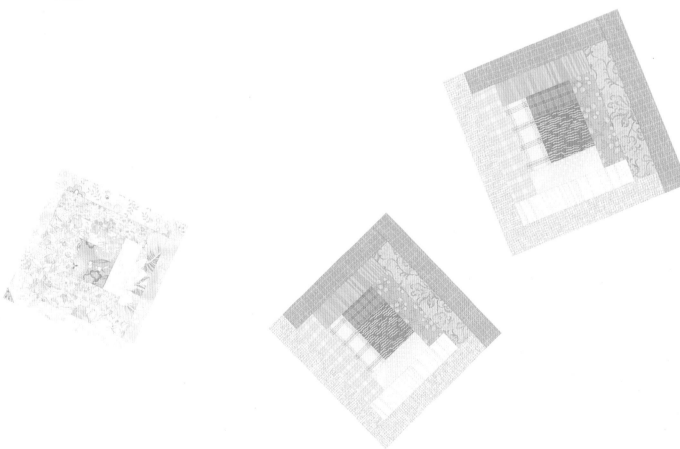

Marta Woodward, model; home of Anne Waterman; Artist Duster, D'Leas Fabric & Button Studio

STARS AND WINDMILLS

Panel: 22" x 33"
Finished Block Size: 5½"
Wendy Hill

Repeat blocks do just this: repeat the same design and color/value placement from block to block. Any Repeat block is a source of color and pattern play. When the blocks are joined, a secondary pattern emerges. If you change the color/value placement you'll have an entirely different looking quilt. See pages 62, 63, 69, 72, and 73 for other examples of Repeat blocks.

Compare the two sides of this twenty-four Repeat block panel: on the yellow/brown side stars are prominent; on the slate blue/brown side, windmill blades stand out.

Detail of block panel—yellow/brown side

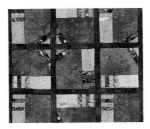

Detail of block panel—blue/brown side

I used the panel to cut out the back yoke of the commercial coat pattern. The coat was assembled around the yoke so the garment would be reversible. I used the facings as decorative bands to finish the coat fronts and back. Cotton batting with scrim was used in the yoke only; the other pattern pieces have no middle layer. The coat is very drapey and comfortable.

Make your own garment with this Repeat block or make something else: place mats, a table runner, a wall quilt, or a bed quilt. Decide what you want to make; use the block pattern as is or enlarge it. Make as many blocks as you need, but remember to adjust the supply list accordingly. Your imagination has no limit!

Color Scheme

The two color schemes share a warm brown color, but are otherwise very different from each other. The lined side features components of a line of jacquard woven Japanese fabrics and a jacquard woven rayon fabric. Jacquard looms are used to make intricately woven fabrics. This unlikely assortment of prints and solids look beautiful together despite—or because of—the riot of colors and textures.

The plain side is the opposite; a small range of colors was used, all of which accent the understated but rich panel of commercial hand-dyed cotton fabric. The coat fronts were surface stitched with a variety of rayon threads to bring out both the colors in the hand-dyed fabric, as well as the silk and cotton fabrics used in the back yoke.

Fabric Selection Tips

Any type of fabric is fair game when making quilts, clothing, and other items that won't be taking trips through the washer and dryer. Try shopping at good quality fashion fabric stores and look around for silks, rayons, and other unusual fabrics. Don't turn your back on slinky, slippery, or very lightweight fabrics. These can be tamed and strengthened with fusible tricot-knit or very light-weight non-woven fusible interfacing. Use the fused fabrics as you would any other similar weight fabrics in your next project.

Supply List

For a Pieced Panel (22" by 33")

Lined side—yellow/brown

Big piece: $1/2$ yard

Five companion pieces: $1/4$ yard each

Plain side—slate blue/brown

Big piece: $1/2$ yard

Five companion pieces: $1/4$ yard each

Tubes: $5/8$ yard

OTHER SUPPLIES

Cotton batting with scrim—cut twenty-four $6^{1}/_{2}$" squares.

Heat-activated transfer pen—any color except white

Favorite marking pen or pencil—with a sharp point

Template plastic or lightweight cardboard —7" square

One sheet of graph paper—at least 7" square

Rotary cutter/mat/grid ruler

Walking foot

Directions

For a Pieced Panel—22" by 33"

1. Plan ahead for your quilt with a sketch or mock block showing fabric placement on both sides.

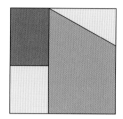

Lined side—yellow/brown

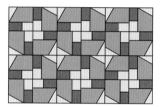

Lined side layout—yellow/brown

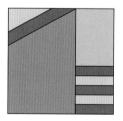

Plain side—blue/brown

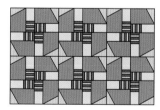

Plain side layout—blue/brown

2. Draft or photocopy a master block

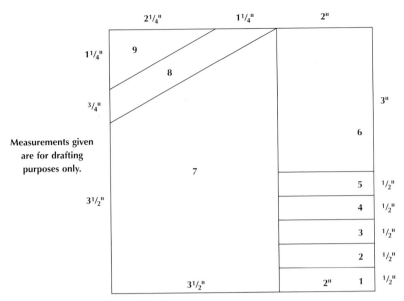

Master block—enlarge to 5$^1/_2$", 200%

Measurements given are for drafting purposes only.

3. Prepare twenty-four foundation blocks using cotton batting with scrim. Trim off the excess batting on the outside seam line; use a grid ruler for accuracy.

4. Prewash fabrics if needed.

5. Precut fabrics.

Lined side

Combination Piece 1-5—cut twenty-four 3" by 3$^1/_2$" pieces.

Piece 6—cut twenty-four 3" by 4" pieces.

Piece 7—cut twenty-four 4$^1/_2$" by 6$^1/_2$" pieces.

Combination Piece 8-9—cut three strips each 3"-wide.

Plain side

Individual Pieces 1-5—cut into strips 1$^1/_4$"-wide.

Piece 6—cut twenty-four 3" by 4" pieces.

Piece 7—cut twenty-four 4$^1/_2$" by 6$^1/_2$" pieces.

Piece 8—cut three strips, each 1$^5/_8$"-wide.

Piece 9—cut two strips, each 2"-wide.

6. Make a template for only Pieces 6, 7, and Combination Piece 8-9; discard the other pieces.

7. Pieces 1-5 are assembled using a variation of the basic technique, "more piecing on one side, substitute a combination piece on the other side." The first five pieces are assembled on the plain side using the marked lines, and then a big piece, Combination Piece 1-5, is substituted on the lined side.

Grade the seams and iron-up with each additional fabric piece.

8. Use the basic technique and template to sew Piece 6 on both

sides. Grade seams and iron-up both sides.

9. Use the basic technique and template to sew Piece 7 on both sides. Grade the seams and iron-up both sides.

10. Use the template to sew Piece 8, plain side and combination Piece 8-9, lined side. Grade the seams.

11. Iron-up Piece 8, plain side only. Use the marked lines to sew Piece 9, plain side. Iron-up Piece 9 and Combination Piece 8-9.

12. Repeat Steps 7-11 to make twenty-three more blocks.

13. Square up the blocks with a 3$/_8$" seam allowance to 6$^1/_4$" and zigzag the edges.

14. Assemble the panel using the block-to-block method, with the lined side, yellow/brown, sewn right sides together. Sew blocks into rows and the rows into a quilt top, using a 3$/_8$" seam allowance. Iron the seams open; whipstitch the seams down.

15. Make tubes—five 3$/_4$"-wide by 23"-long and three 3$/_4$"-wide by 34"-long. Center the tubes over the seams and blindstitch in place. Attach the shorter tubes first, then the longer tubes, or weave them (over, under) as I did. If making a bigger or smaller panel, adjust the length and quantity of the tubes as needed to cover up the seams.

Personality Nametag by Wendy Hill

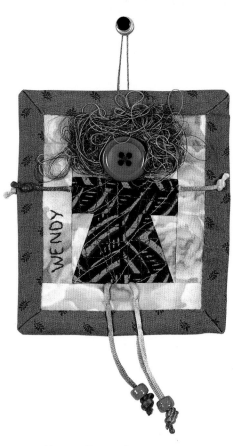

Alternate Personality (nametag)

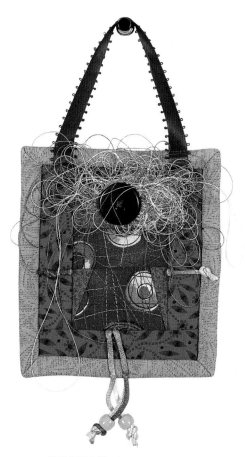

Wild Child by Krista Garrison

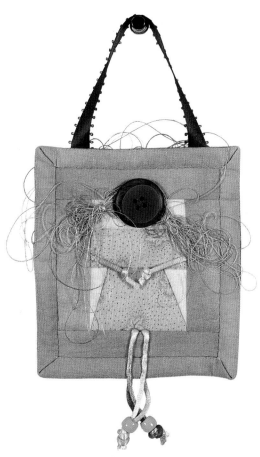

Sophisticated Girl

Representational blocks depict objects of all sorts in a recognizable way, such as animals, plants, hearts, butterflies, boats, planes, houses, and on and on. There are abundant resources of patterns for foundation-pieced Representational blocks. Look for blocks foundation pieced from start to finish; patterns with pre-pieced sections are fine. Avoid blocks foundation pieced in units and then assembled. These seams must be covered up and often make the block unusable for reversible-foundation piecing. For another example of a Representational block, see page 66.

NAMETAG AND WILD CHILD/ SOPHISTICATED GIRL

4" x 4³/₄"
Krista Garrison and Wendy Hill

I couldn't resist making reversible Button Babies, this time as a block. My young neighbor, Krista, made a tiny wall hanging for her bedroom while I made a cute nametag. It was fun sewing with a twelve-year-old, and Krista was able to use the templates to do her own pinning, marking, and sewing. Try making these blocks with your own young relatives, friends or as a school/club project. Use the blocks for nametags, wall hangings, or connect the blocks with sashing for a cute "paper doll" wall hanging.

Supply List for One Button Baby Block

Dress: Two each 4" x 4"

Background 1: Two each 4" x 4"

Background 2: Two each 6" x 6"

One-fabric binding: about 4" by 22"

Two-fabric binding: two fabrics, each about 3" x 22"

Rattail cording: 1 yard—cut four 2¹/₂" lengths and four 4¹/₂" lengths.

Barrel beads: two

Ribbon—wall hanging only: about ¹/₄ yard

Embroidery thread—nametag only: about 18"

Assorted spools of thread—for hair

Buttons: two about ¹/₂" to ³/₄" diameter—any shape

Batting: 5" by 6"

Non-woven, lightweight fusible interfacing: 4³/₄" by 5³/₄"

Heat-activated transfer pen—any color except white

Favorite marking pen or pencil with a sharp point

Template plastic or lightweight cardboard

One sheet of graph paper (at least 6" square)

Rotary cutter/mat/grid ruler

Walking foot

Fabric Selection Tips

Just about anything goes with these little blocks. Look through your fabric scraps or stash for colors to suit your mood, personality, career, or to match the season or holidays. Express yourself with your choice of clothing, button, and hairstyle. Be sure to choose fabrics with good color contrast so that the dress can be distinguished from the background.

Directions

1. Plan ahead with a sketch or mock blocks showing fabric placement for both sides. Refer to the drawings for guidance.

2. Trace or photocopy a master block.

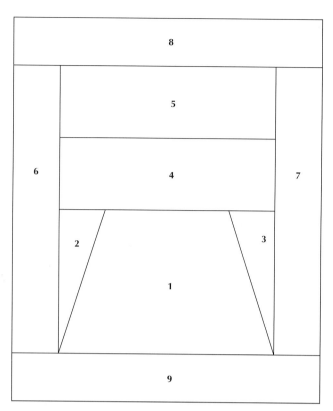

Master block 3¹/₄" x 4"

3. Prepare the foundation block(s) using batting and interfacing. If making only one Button Baby, hand trace the pattern directly onto the interfacing. Trim off excess batting, leaving a ³/₈" seam allowance around the outside seam line.

4. Make templates: You'll need Pieces 2-9.

5. Prewash, precut, and organize the fabrics. Knot the ends of the shorter lengths of rattail, the arms.

6. Use the basic technique to construct the block. Before sewing Pieces 6 and 7 to the block, center the shorter lengths of rattail over Piece 4 and tape in place. In the same way, position and tape the legs over Piece 1 before sewing Piece 9 to the block.

7. Square up the block(s) even with the batting—do not accidentally amputate appendages! Zigzag the edges.

8. If using a ribbon loop, place it right sides together along the top edge (on the appropriate side) about 1" from the corners. The ribbon will be sandwiched in the seam between the quilt-block and the binding.

9. Use a single-fabric or two-fabric/double French-fold binding to finish the edges. Keep the arms and legs out of the seam. If using a loop, push up the ribbon loop and finger-press to flatten it out. Machine stitch the loop to the binding, using matching thread, just below where the binding folds over. Blindstitch the binding in place, mitering the corners.

10. The arms may be left in place, looking as though they are folded; see the pastel side of SOPHISTICATED GIRL/WILD CHILD. To make the arms outstretched, couch the rattail with monofiliment thread. Hold the legs in place the same way. String a barrel bead on both pairs of legs (front and back together) and knot the ends. Let the legs fall as they will.

11. Gather up a handful of thread to "style" the hair for both sides. Center the styled hair over Piece 5, cover with a button, and sew the button in place. Using the same needle and thread, center the hair over Piece 5 on the opposite side, and sew the button in place; go through the holes in both buttons, back and forth.

12. For nametags, hand-embroider or use a permanent pen to write your name along the side of the block. Attach a braided thread loop to the center, top edge of the binding. Hang the thread loop over a button on your clothing or pin the thread loop to your clothing.

Tree A—Spring Side

Tree B—Winter Side

Tree B—Spring Side

Tree A—Winter Side

ONE BY ONE

Each: 6³/₄" x 7³/₄"
Finished Block Size: 6" by 7"
Lila Krause and Wendy Hill

These diminutive wall hangings
are perfect for anyone who:

1. Needs a thirty-six hour day.

2. Wants to make a gift but doesn't
have enough time—see 1.

3. Likes to start and finish projects
in one day—see 1.

4. Loves wall hangings, but hasn't
finished one yet—see 1.

Make one or a series to scatter,
cluster, or strew around the walls
for the holidays or anytime of
year. After making these patterns,
take a new look at other representational foundation-pieced patterns for more one-block wall
hangings. They are "sew" easy, you
can even give them away.

House B—Winter Side

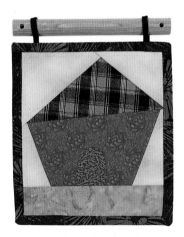

House A—Spring Side

House B—Spring Side

House A—Winter Side

Tree C—Spring Side

Tree C—Winter Side

Color Scheme

Lila chose seasonal colors for this set of five, one block wall hangings. As she looked through the pile of fabrics, she sorted those with a fresh, spring/summer look into one pile, and those with a wintry, snowy look into another pile. Lila sorted through the fabrics again, looking for colors and textures to evoke the feeling of a tree trunk, snow on the ground, roofing, grass, color of the sky and so on. Once the fabrics were selected, Lila made small mock blocks to help keep the colors straight.

Supply List

FOR ONE HOUSE BLOCK

Body of house: Two each 6" by 8"

Roof: Two each 4" by 8"

Door: Two each 2$\frac{1}{2}$" by 3"

Chimney—winter side only: 2" by 2"

Sky: Two each 9" by 9"

Grass/ground: Two each 4" by 8"

FOR ONE TREE BLOCK

Body of tree: Two each 8" by 9"

Trunk: Two each 3" by 4"

Grass/ground: 4" by 8"

Sky: Two each 9" by 9"

OTHER SUPPLIES FOR ONE BLOCK

Batting: 8" by 9"

Non-woven, lightweight fusible interfacing: 7$\frac{3}{4}$" by 8$\frac{3}{4}$"

Heat-activated transfer pen —any color except white

Binding, Fabric 1: cut one strip 1" by 36".

Binding, Fabric 2: cut one strip 1$\frac{7}{8}$" by 36".

Loops: about 10" per block, self-made or purchased narrow $\frac{1}{2}$"-wide bias.

Favorite marking pen or pencil—with a sharp point

Template plastic or lightweight cardboard

Graph paper: One sheet per block—at least 8" by 9"

Rotary cutter/mat/grid ruler

Walking foot

Half round dowels: $\frac{3}{4}$" diameter or smaller, by 6$\frac{3}{4}$" long

TIP

Quilters often work with small, precut pieces of fabric, but the fabric is purchased from big bolts. It's important to "view" the fabric the way it will be used: how will a small piece look when taken out of the context of the larger expansive pattern? Make an assortment of "reverse" templates: cardboard or plastic frames with different shaped cutout holes. Take these templates along on your next fabric shopping trip and look at the bolts the way you'll actually be using the fabrics.

Directions

1. Plan ahead with a sketch or mock blocks to show fabric placement for both sides. Refer to the graph drawings for guidance.

2. Photocopy a master block.

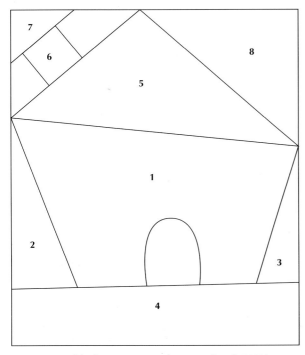

Master block, House A—enlarge to 6" x 7", 200%.

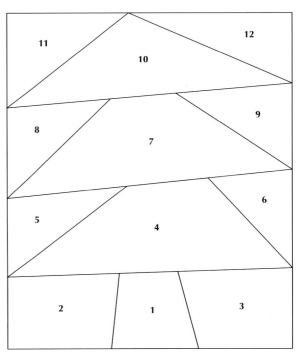

Master block, Tree A—Tree C—enlarge to 6" x 7", 200%.

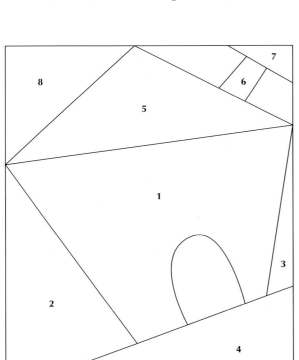

Master block, House B—enlarge to 6" x 7", 200%.

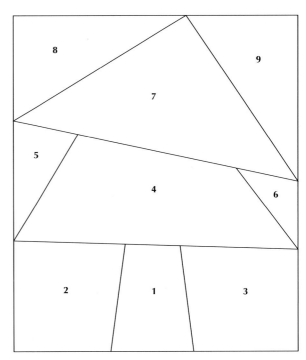

Master block, Tree B—enlarge to 6" x 7", 200%.

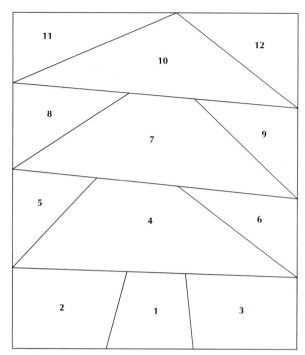

Master block, Tree C—enlarge to 6" x 7", 200%.

3. Prepare one foundation block with batting and interfacing per wall hanging. Trim off excess batting, leaving a $3/8$" seam allowance beyond the outside seam line on all sides.

4. Make templates for each different pattern you plan to make.

5. Prewash precut and organize fabrics.

6. Use the basic technique for the block assembly. Grade the seams and iron-up the pieces with each additional fabric piece.

HOUSES ONLY

If using the chimney on one side of the house blocks, pre-piece the chimney using strips of fabric: sky, chimney, and sky. Use the template Combination Piece 6-7 to position and sew the pre-pieced chimney Piece 6, plain side and the Combination Piece 6-7 lined side. Iron-up the chimney piece only. Use the marked line to position and sew Piece 7, plain side. Iron-up Piece 7, plain side and the Combination Piece 6-7, lined side. Trace and cut out a door piece with $3/16$" seam allowance added. Blindstitch in place onto the block.

FINISH ASSEMBLING THE BLOCK

7. Square-up the blocks, cutting off excess fabric along the edge of the batting. Zigzag the edges.

8. Make the loops by folding over the $1/2$" bias strip and topstitching along both sides. Place the loops along the right side of the top edge about 1" from the corners of the quilt. The loops will be sandwiched in the seam between the quilt top and the binding.

9. Make a two-fabric/double French-fold binding. Position and pin the narrow side right sides together with the appropriate side of the quilt. Use a $3/8$" seam allowance, miter at each corner, miter the ends and finish the seam.

10. Open out the binding along the top edge. Push up the loops and finger-press to flatten them out a bit. Machine stitch the loop to the binding, with matching thread, just below the seam line between the two fabrics. This strengthens and holds the loops in place.

11. Fold the binding over at the seam line between the two fabrics. Blindstitch the binding in place, mitering at the corners.

Marta Woodward, model; home of Anne Waterman; East Meets West #13046,
Fabric Collections & Cutting Corners

Roses/and More Roses

Panel 37" x 63"
Finished block size: 5" by 5"
Laura Clark and Wendy Hill

Crazy quilt blocks have long been a way to use up small scraps of quilts. Many early Crazy quilt blocks were constructed from odd pieces of fabrics placed helter-skelter onto a fabric base, then blind-stitched in place. The fabrics could be curved around to make them fit and cover raw edges. Often embroidery with assorted threads and ribbons embellished the blocks.

A foundation-pieced Crazy Quilt block must use straight seams sewn in a sequence. This block is constructed similarly to a Log Cabin block, with successive pieces added irregularly around a starting point. My Crazy Quilt block is a chameleon; it can look like roses, a stylized kind of flower, or nothing like a flower at all, depending on fabric choices—see page 77 for another use of this block.

The original plan for this project called for seventy-two reverse-pieced Crazy Quilt rose blocks. After piecing just one block, Laura and I knew the plans had to be modified. The new, revised plan with just twenty-seven pieced blocks unexpectedly improved the overall design. Adversity can be an opportunity for something even better! We connected the blocks with sashing to make a large panel.

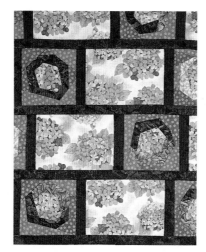

Detail of large panel—lined side

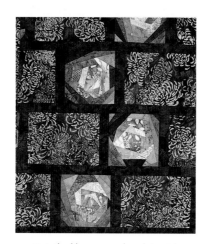

Detail of large panel—plain side

The panel could have been used as a wall hanging or bed quilt, but for this sample it was cut up to make a no side-seam kimono coat. The uninterrupted pattern piece (front, back, and front) provides a canvas to display these beautiful pieced blocks. Use the project directions to make a panel of your own for a quilt or clothing or anything your heart desires. Adjust the given fabric amounts to make a larger or smaller panel as needed for your project.

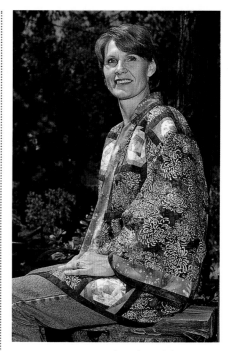

Marta Woodward, model; home of Anne Waterman

Color Scheme

The Rose side of the coat combines purple and yellow, complementary—or opposite—colors on the color wheel. In full strength, complementary colors can "vibrate". These colors, although bright, are viewer friendly. The mix of pinks and peach with the yellows softens the clash with purple. The variety of greens in the leaves, an analogous mix of everything from acid green, to grass green, peacock, teal, forest green, and olive, gives the eye another place to look.

The other side, And More Roses, features another complementary color scheme: blue-green and red-orange. The mix of teal, green, and blue fabrics with a burnt orange, instead of a pure red-orange, softens the clash of the complimentary colors. Other colors—pink, yellow-orange, caramel, and gold—add to the mix in a pleasant way.

Supply List

For a Pieced Panel
37" by 63"

ROSE SIDE—PLAIN SIDE

Assorted greens: Seven colors—1/4 yard each

Assorted rose petals: Ten colors—1/4 yard each

Plain, unpieced blocks: 1 yard—cut twenty-seven 5³/₄" by 7³/₄" rectangles.

Sashing: 2 yards

AND MORE ROSES SIDE—LINED SIDE

Flower fabric to cut individually: need twenty-seven blooms about 3" by 3" finished.

Companion fabrics for petals: Four different fabrics, each ³/₈ yard

Leaf fabrics: Two different fabrics, each ³/₄ yard

Plain, unpieced blocks: 1 yard—cut twenty-seven 5³/₄" by 7³/₄" rectangles.

Sashing: 2 yards

OTHER SUPPLIES

Non-woven nylon: one roll Sulky Soft 'n Sheer or enough to cut out twenty-seven 5" squares and twenty-seven 5³/₄" by 7³/₄" rectangles.

Heat-activated transfer pen—any color except white

Favorite marking pen or pencil—with a sharp point

Template plastic or lightweight cardboard

One sheet of graph paper—at least 6" square

Rotary cutter/mat/grid ruler

Walking foot

Directions

1. Plan ahead with a sketch or mock blocks showing fabric placement for both sides.

Lined side

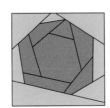

Plain side

2. Trace or photo copy the master block.

3. Prepare twenty-seven foundation blocks using non-woven nylon stabilizer. Trim off the excess fabric on the outside seam line using a grid ruler for accuracy.

4. Make a set of templates for these pieces: 1-6 combination, 7, 8, 9, 10, 11, 12, 13, 14,15, 16-17 combination, 18-20 combination, 21-23 combination, and 24-26 combination.

5. Prewash the fabrics. Precut all the block fabrics, except the fussy cut flower, into big chunks, such as 6" by 13". As you sew each piece to the foundation block, cut off excess fabric leaving a generous seam allowance around the shape of each piece. Fussy cut twenty-seven flowers individually 3¹/₂" square for the lined side centers.

6. Use a variation of the basic technique to assemble the Crazy Quilt blocks, with more piecing on the plain side and substituting combination pieces on the lined side. Grade the seams and iron-up with each additional fabric piece. Starting on the lined side, use the marked lines to foundation piece the first six pieces on the plain side. Substitute the Combination piece 1-6 on the lined side; this is the individually cut flower.

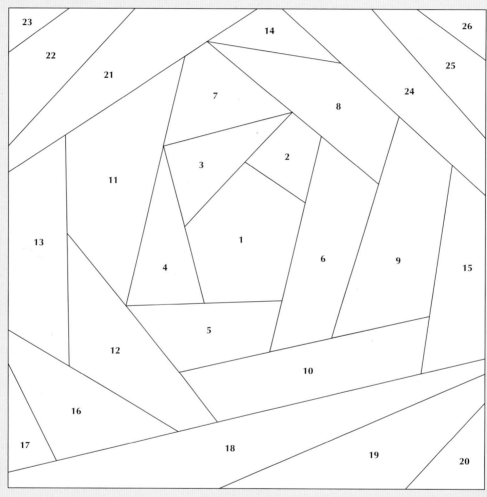

5" x 5" master block

7. Follow the basic technique to reverse piece the next nine Pieces, 7, 8, 9, 10, 11, 12, 13, 14, and 15 on both sides.

8. Use the same variation of the basic technique to add Piece 16 (plain side) and the Combination Piece 16-17, lined side. Iron-up Piece 16, plain side only. Add Piece 17, plain side, using the marked lines on the lined side. Iron-up both Piece 17 and the Combination Piece 16-17.

9. Use the same variation of the basic technique to add Piece 18, plain side and the Combination Piece 18-20, lined side. Iron-up Piece 18, plain side only. Add Piece 19, plain side and iron-up. Add Piece 20, plain side. Iron-up both Piece 20 and the Combination Piece 18-20.

10. Use the same variation of the basic technique to add Piece 21, plain side and the Combination Piece 21-23, lined side. Iron-up Piece 21, plain side only. Add Piece 22, plain side, and iron-up. Add Piece 23, plain side. Iron-up both Piece 23 and the Combination Piece 21-23.

11. Use the same variation of the basic technique to add Piece 24, plain side, and the Combination Piece 24-26, lined side. Iron-up Piece 24, plain side only. Add Piece 25, plain side, and iron-up. Add Piece 26, plain side. Iron-up both Piece 26 and the Combination Piece 24-26.

12. Repeat to make twenty-six more blocks. To speed the process along, work on a group of six or so blocks at a time. Do the entire pin-poking, pinning, marking, sewing, trimming, and ironing to the group of blocks in an assembly-line fashion.

13. Square up the blocks with a $3/8$" seam allowance—$5^3/4$" total.

PANEL ASSEMBLY

1. Cut both sashing fabrics into thirteen strips each, parallel with the selvage: $1^3/4$" wide by length of fabric. Cut six strips of both color schemes into sixty $5^3/4$" sashing pieces. Set aside seven fabric strips each of both color schemes for the long sashing strips.

2. Pair and stack the plain rectangle blocks wrong sides together, with the nylon stabilizer in the middle. Baste or zigzag edges.

3. Assemble the blocks into rows with the short sashing, starting and stopping with the sashing.

The seam allowance fills the space of the sashing so no additional nylon needs to be added. Blindstitch the free edge of the sashing in place.

4. Assemble the rows into a panel with the sashing, starting and stopping with the sashing, refer to the layout diagram. The rows are "jogged" back and forth a little bit to avoid straight vertical sashing strip lines running through the panel. The seam allowance fills the space; no additional nylon is needed. Blindstitch the free edge of the sashing in place.

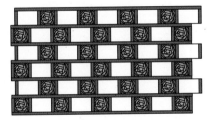

Layout diagram

USE THE PANEL

The panel is now ready to be used. For clothing, cut out the pattern pieces and assemble the garment, making it reversible around the panel pieces. For a quilt, bind the edges with a single-fabric or two-fabric/double French-fold binding See Binding page 79.

Sixteen Turkish Beauties

Four Square Butterflies

Project Seven: Fan Blocks

Fan blocks, used in quiltmaking throughout history, are found in countless variations. Almost all fan blocks have a quarter circle in one corner (sometimes two opposite corners) and pieces which radiate from the same corner. Fan blocks are pieced in units: the background piece, one or more arcs, and the quarter circle. The arcs themselves may be pieced with pointed spires or straight edged blades or left plain; some fan patterns have pieced quarter circles too.

All sorts of Fan blocks lend themselves to reversible-foundation piecing. The various arcs and quarter circles are reverse pieced first, then connected together with the background piece. One side is sewn right sides together. The exposed seams on the other side are covered up with bias trim or ribbons, adding to the natural design of the block. Here is a project using Fan blocks with pieced and plain arcs. See pages 64, 65 and 75 for other examples of reverse-pieced fan blocks.

SIXTEEN TURKISH BEAUTIES/FOUR SQUARE BUTTERFLIES

65$\frac{1}{2}$" x 65$\frac{1}{2}$"
Finished Block Size: 15"
Debra Wruck

The oversized blocks make it easy to sew, and only sixteen blocks make a good size quilt. Debra's block design features three arcs, two of which are pieced. The outer arc has more piecing on one side than the other, reducing the total piecing a bit, and giving the two sides an even greater difference in look.

NOTE:
Debra used the same fabric (lined side) for the outer and inner arc spires, sashing and binding and self-made bias trim, for a total of 6$\frac{1}{4}$ yards.

TIP

Debra is a big fan of making mock blocks, both on paper and on the computer. When working on the computer, she scans the fabric into the computer or downloads the fabric straight from the company websites. The colors are realistic, she can change fabrics with a click, and she can print her finished mock blocks. Other times Debra constructs mock blocks with actual fabric snips, paper and glue stick. She enjoys the physical handling of the fabrics and the pleasant time spent musing over fabric choices.

Supply List

LINED SIDE—BUTTERFLIES

Block background piece: 4 yards

Outer and inner arc spires, sashing, and binding: 4 yards

Middle plain arc, quarter circle, and sashing square: $3/4$ yard

Inner arc background: $1\frac{1}{2}$ yards

Outer arc background: 2 yards

Purchased $1/2$"-wide bias tape: 44 yards

PLAIN SIDE—TURKISH BEAUTIES

Block background piece: 4 yards

Outer arc background: 2 yards

Outer pieced arc Spire 1 and quarter circle: $1\frac{1}{2}$ yards

Outer pieced arc Spire 2, inner arc spire, sashing, and binding: $3\frac{3}{4}$ yards

Center plain arc: $1/2$ yard

Inner arc background and sashing square: $1\frac{1}{2}$ yards

OTHER SUPPLIES

Batting: 80" by 80"

Non-woven, lightweight fusible interfacing: 4 yards

Heat-activated transfer pen—any color except white

Freezer paper

Rotary cutter/mat/grid ruler

Walking foot

Dowel: one $3/4$" in diameter by 66" long

Directions

1. Plan ahead for your quilt with a sketch or mock blocks showing fabric placement for both sides.

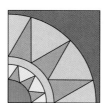

Lined side

Plain side—after piecing

2. Photocopy a master block and cut the sections apart. Prepare thirty-two foundation blocks, arc shapes only, using batting and fusible interfacing. Trim off excess batting on the outside seam line.

3. Prewash fabrics.

TEMPLATES

Background, quarter circle, and center plain arc templates: make one template with the $1/4$" seam allowance included. Make one finished size template with no seam allowance for background and quarter circle. Spires and background pieces for the two pieced arcs: make templates with a generous $1/2$" added around all sides.

Make templates out of freezer paper to precut the fabrics. Lightly press the freezer paper to the fabric; use sharp scissors or a rotary cutter to cut out the fabrics. Peel off the freezer paper and use again.

PRECUTTING GUIDE

Background Pieces, Middle Plain Arc, and Quarter Circle/Fabric: use the template with seam allowance added—sixteen each, both sides.

Background Pieces and Quarter Circle/Batting: use the finished size template, no seam allowance included—cut sixteen each total.

Outer pieced arc/lined side
Combination spire—cut forty-eight.

Background pieces—cut sixty-four.

Outer pieced arc/plain side
Double spires—cut forty-eight, each color.

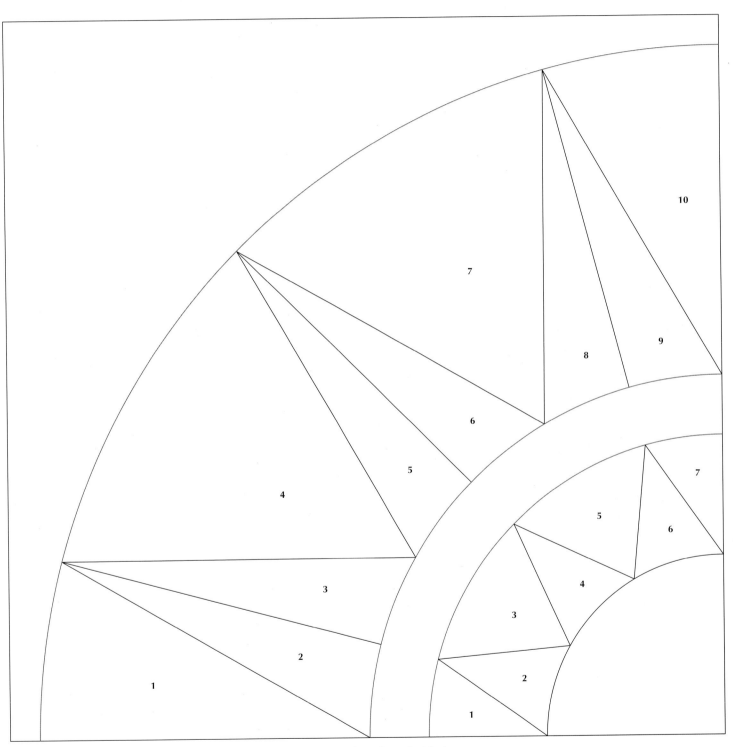

*Master block—enlarge the block
pattern to 15" square, 200%.*

Background pieces—cut sixty-four.

Inner pieced arc

Spires—cut forty-eight, each side.

Background pieces—cut sixty-four, each side.

Directions

Inner arc

1. The inner pieced arc just uses the no-template variation. With this method, each seam is sewn twice, first positioning the numbered piece on the plain side and sewing on the marked line on the lined side; then positioning the same numbered piece on the lined side and sewing over the stitched line on the plain side. Remember to get started with Piece 1 and 2 before adding successive pieces. Grade the seams and iron-up.

2. Reverse-piece sixteen inner arcs. Square-up the arcs. Machine-baste or zigzag the outside edges.

Outer Arc

The outer arc has twin spires on the plain side and a combination, single, spire on the lined side.

Use the no template, one-sided foundation piecing and the more piecing one side; substitute combination piece other side variations of the basic technique to assemble the outer pieced arc.

1. Using the pin-poke method, position and pin Pieces 1 and 2 on the plain side. From the lined side, stitch the first seam along the marked line.

2. Position and pin Pieces 1 and Combination Piece 2-3 on the lined side. From the plain side, stitch the seam AGAIN, stitching over the first stitched seam line. Grade the seams on both sides.

3. Iron-up Piece 2 on the PLAIN side only.

4. Pin-poke the next seam line. Position and pin Piece 3 on the plain side. From the lined side, stitch the seam line. Be sure to keep Combination Piece 2-3, lined side, out of the way. Grade the seam allowance, plain side.

5. Iron-up Piece 3 on the plain side.

6. Pin-poke the next seam line. Position and pin Piece 4 on the plain side. From the lined side, stitch the seam line.

7. Iron-up Combination Piece 2-3 on the lined side. Pin-poke the seam line—using the stitched line, plain side as a guide. Position and pin Piece 4 on the lined side.

8. From the plain side, stitch the seam AGAIN, stitching over the same stitched seam. Grade the seams on both sides.

9. Continue in this manner to finish the arc.

TIP

When reverse piecing the arcs, mark and trim the $1/4$" seam allowance on the plain side as you sew. After the entire arc is pieced, place the arc plain side up. Use the precut edge as a guide to trim of the excess fabrics from the lined side fabrics.

BLOCK ASSEMBLY

1. Sandwich the background pieces and quarter circles with the batting, centering the batting so there is a $1/4$" seam allowance all the way around. Pin or hand-baste to hold the layers together. Machine-baste or zigzag the outside edges using a walking foot, keeping the whole thing flat.

2. Pair up the background piece with the outer arc, right sides together. Match and pin the two pieces in the exact center and the outside edge. Ease the two pieces together and pin closely. Sew with a $1/4$" seam allow-ance. Clip seams if necessary. Iron seam toward background piece.

3. Continue to sew the block parts together as in Step 2 until the block is completed. Repeat to make the remaining fifteen blocks.

4. Square up the blocks with a $1/4$" seam allowance to $15^1/_2$".

5. Cover up the seams with purchased $1/2$"-wide bias strips. Line up the bias strips along the edge of the points. Pin and blindstitch in place.

TIP

Tip for block assembly. If the curve is tight, pin and sew half the curved seam at a time, edge to center, center to edge.

Always pin the pieces together along the sides. This forces the easing to take place along the curved seam where it belongs, and keeps the sides of your block straight.

If the quarter circle is too small to sew comfortably by machine, blindstitch the quarter-circle in place.

6. Cut the sashing strips for both sides—twenty-four pieces, 2" by $15^1/_2$". Cut nine center squares for both sides—2" by 2". Assemble the three horizontal sashing strips for both sides: sashing + square + sashing + square + sashing + square + sashing with $1/4$" seams.

7. Add batting to sashing—refer to page 86. Connect the blocks to the sashing in four rows. Connect the four rows to sashing to complete the quilt top. Blindstitch the free edges of the sashing in place as you go.

8. Make eight two-fabric loops, the size desired for your dowel. Pin right sides together along the top edge of the quilt. The loops will be sandwiched in the seam between the quilt top and the binding.

9. Make a two-fabric/double French-fold binding. Position and pin the narrow fabric right sides together on the appropriate quilt side. Use a $3/_8$" seam allowance, miter at each corner, miter the ends to finish the seam.

10. Open out the binding along the top edge. Push up the loops and finger-press to flatten them out a bit. Machine-stitch the loop to the binding, using matching thread, just below the seam line between the two fabrics. This strengthens and holds the loops in place.

11. Fold the binding over at the seam line between the two fabrics. Blindstitch the binding in place, mitering at the corners. Hang the quilt and enjoy!

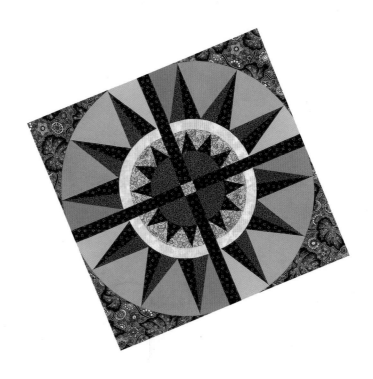

Reversible-foundation piecing is both a method, and an inspiration to try new quilting ideas. The following examples range from traditional to innovative, practical to fantastic, subdued to colorful, providing readers the courage, the heart, and the spirit to try out their own ideas. The recipe is simple: combine your favorite foundation-pieced pattern with any item which can be turned inside-out or flipped over, and add reversible-foundation piecing. You'll be on your way toward making your own reversible masterpiece!

QUILTS

Chasing the Blues—Away

63$\frac{1}{2}$" x 84"
Wendy Hill
Repeat block

The Square-within-a-Square block pattern provides a playground for combining a variety of fabrics and visual textures. Whether constructed in a typical block size or as an overgrown giant of a block, this basic pattern can be found in many sources or easily drafted on your own. This quilt is almost monochromatic on the indigo blue side. The addition of a print with tiny motifs in red, green, yellow, and blue relieves any monotony. The other side is quite the splash with just about every color but blue in the assorted big prints. This would be a good choice for a "his" and "her" type of quilt. Cotton batting was used for the foundation material along with the usual supplies for reversible-foundation piecing, page 8.

Since the 20" blocks are so huge, the block design was hand-traced onto the interfacing with a permanent pen, then the interfacing was fused to the batting. The blocks were assembled following the basic technique. The quilt was put together with sashing and bound with a two-fabric/double French-fold binding.

Make one block for a small wall hanging, four blocks for a larger wall hanging, or keep making blocks to get the size quilt desired. The block does have a lot of pieces but the sewing is only repetitious—not difficult. This is a perfect project for people new to reversible-foundation piecing or for quilters who want to use large numbers of different fabrics.

Home of Sandra Bruce and Gary Pierazzi; model—Matteo Pierazzi

Two by Two

35¹/₂" x 50"
Grace Evans
Repeat block

A new baby granddaughter and a love for trying new things led Grace to make this reversible baby quilt. The title refers both to the two-sided nature of the quilt and the fabrics with animal and Noah's Ark themes. Grace used cotton batting along with the usual supplies for reversible-foundation piecing, page 8.

At first it seems impossible to believe the two sides of this quilt were sewn simultaneously through one batt. Grace achieved the magic of the two different looks

by pre-piecing the four-patch on the Snail's Trail side and using one big square for the other side. Otherwise, she followed the basic technique quite closely. Grace made her tubes with fabric and fusible interfacing. She sewed the bumpy side of the interfacing to the right side of the fabric, and turned the tube right side out. Fusing the tubes in place, instead of pinning, Grace then blind-stitched them in place.

Grace is a "topper", a person who would rather make tops than finish the quilt. She loves the way the quilt is completely finished after the blocks are assembled. She is not a fan of hand-sewing, but she felt it paid off by getting two-quilts-in-one. For advice, Grace reminds readers to cut the pieces generously oversized and recommends practicing with a Log Cabin block before trying other patterns.

Old Timey/Victorian Heyday

22" x 26"
Wendy Hill
Fan block

This tiny bed quilt is just the right size for a 20" doll. One side looks old fashioned with nine narrow fan blades, two tiny print flannels for the block, and two soft beige plaids for the sashing. The other side is reminiscent of the Victorian era and the tendency toward excess, with three wide fan blades, hand-dyed commercial fabrics, silk fabrics, thread embellishment, and fancy trims.

I followed a variation of the basic technique with more piecing on one side and substituted a combination piece on the other side. Just the arc was used for the foundation block with wool batting and lightweight fusible interfacing. Other supplies include the usual assortment for reversible-foundation piecing, page 8.

The block pieces were sewn together to complete the blocks. The Old Timey side was assembled right sides together using just the background and the quarter circle pieces. For added glitz on the Victorian side, I grid quilted

the background and quarter circle fabrics. The pieces butted up against the arc. I covered the seams with purchased trims. The blocks were assembled with sashing, and the outside edge was finished with a two-fabric ruffle.

Victorian Heyday

Old Timey

Asia Meets Africa

35¹/₂" x 35¹/₂"
Finished block size: 16¹/₂"
Debra Wruck
Fan block

Debra has a fascination for Fan blocks, particularly the New York Beauty type, because the design possibilities are so infinite. Debra decided to make the blocks very large to simplify the joining of the units. With a love for color, she was easily inspired by the fabrics on the Asia side and intrigued with colors and textures of the fabrics for the Africa side.

Debra used cotton batting along with the usual assortment of supplies for reversible foundation piecing, page 8. She blindstitched self-made bias strips in place to cover up the seams. The blocks were joined with sashing. Binding finishes the edges and the giant loops with buttons are used to hang the quilt.

Heart to Heart

Social Butterflies

Social Butterflies/ Heart to Heart

37" x 51"
Sue McMahan and Wendy Hill
Representational block

Here is a simple quilt with butterflies on one side and hearts on the other. The imagery is boosted by the color choices. Strong black and white geometrics were chosen for the butterfly wings, while candy-colored, saturated pastels were selected for the hearts. The quilt required the usual assortment of supplies for reversible-foundation piecing, page 8.

This reverse-foundation piecing is done on two separate units; the units are joined to make one block. For each unit, the butterfly "wings" have two pieces, while the "heart" side has one piece. Using a variation of the basic technique to sew more pieces on one side and substituting a combination piece on the other side, the wings were assembled first on the plain side. A single piece of heart fabric was placed on the lined side, with the remaining background pieces for both sides added in sequence following the basic technique

The units were squared-up and sewn right sides together on the heart side. The butterfly "body" and matching background fabric strips form natural cover-ups for the seam. Couched black chenille antennas complete the butterfly look. The blocks were assembled with sashing by machine and finished with a single-fabric/double French-fold binding. Loops sewn into the binding allow the quilt to be hung from a dowel.

This quilt would make a cute wall hanging for a baby's room or could be made larger for a bed quilt for an older child (one who wouldn't be tempted to chew off the antennas). The small number of pieces per block makes the piecing go fast, but extra attention to accuracy is required so the hearts and wings line up properly when the units are assembled.

Spyra Gyra

44 1/4" x 44 1/4"
Wendy Hill
Log Cabin block

Fabric choices and placement are critically important with this stunning yet deceptively simple wall quilt using only sixteen blocks. Fabric placement must be planned ahead for both sides and once sewn, the blocks cannot be rotated without breaking up the pattern on the reproduction print side. Making a detailed sketch and mock blocks for both sides of the quilt was necessary to keep everything straight during block assembly.

The pattern is a basic Log Cabin with four logs on one side and eight logs on the reverse side. Two variations of the basic technique were used: more piecing on one side, substitute a combination piece on the other side and more piecing on one side with visible quilting on the other side. The bobbin thread was allowed to show in certain areas but not in others. Many references to the detailed sketch and notes were necessary.

Log Cabin blocks are easy enough for the beginner quilter, but their infinite capacity for color and pattern play could provide one quilter enough diversion for a lifetime of making quilts. For the quilter who loves planning ahead, this is the type of reversible-foundation-piecing project for you.

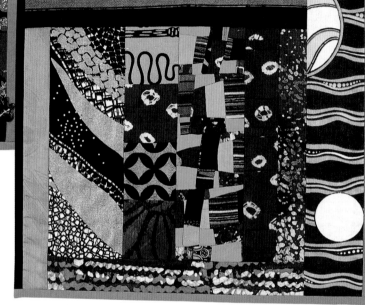

Tawnya's

18½" x 16½"
Tawnya G. Romig-Foster
Strip-Pieced pattern

Tawnya enjoys free-form quilting, so she used a deceptively simple process to make a complicated looking "one block" wall hanging. Although the body of the quilt is simply five long reverse-pieced rectangle-shaped strips, Tawnya pre-pieced many of the strips for added texture and interest. The pre-pieced strips include both geometric and random shapes and are used just like whole-cloth pieces of fabric during the assembly process.

To assemble the quilt, Tawnya followed the basic technique. After reverse-piecing the five panels together, the borders were reverse-pieced Log Cabin style, starting on one side and adding the next three borders in succession. The binding was added the same way, starting with the navy blue fabric and ending with the green fabric. Tawnya uses wooden quilt clamps to hang this quilt.

Tawnya would like to credit workshop teachers Roberta Horton and Kumiko Sudo, friends Christine Drumright and Wendy Hill, and her family for always being her cheerleaders. When asked for advice, Tawnya says: "Do what you love and keep it simple!"

"...and the heavens and the earth."(Genesis 1:1)

21" x 21"
Karla Rogers
Repeat block

Karla used a traditional pattern known as "Sweet Gum Leaf" for her small wall hanging; first published in 1895 by the Ladies Art Company and compiled in the *Encyclopedia of Pieced Quilt Patterns* by Barbara Brackman, published by American Quilter's Society, 1993. She was first inspired by the fabrics, then became intrigued with the idea of the star type pattern on one side contrasting

with the garden look on the other side. Other materials included cotton batting, rayon threads, and the usual assortment of supplies for reversible-foundation piecing, page 8.

Karla followed the basic technique to reverse piece and assemble the sixteen 4" blocks. To enhance the garden look on the "earth" side of the quilt, Karla used the fabric tubes to make a "trellis" as she covered the seams. She embellished the trellis with three folded fabric flowers and leaves. Karla surface stitched the border fabric with selected thread colors to compliment each side. The borders were

connected with a narrow border, handstitched on one side. A single-fabric/double French-fold binding finishes the wall hanging, with matching loops for hanging the quilt.

Karla has several hints for others just beginning to work with reversible-foundation-pieced projects: choose a simple block design and use the templates, because you won't save time trying to avoid them. Make sure the block is big enough to look good after the seams are covered up with fabric tubes; if not, consider using sashing to connect the blocks.

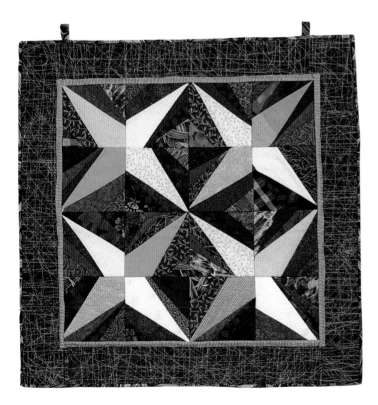

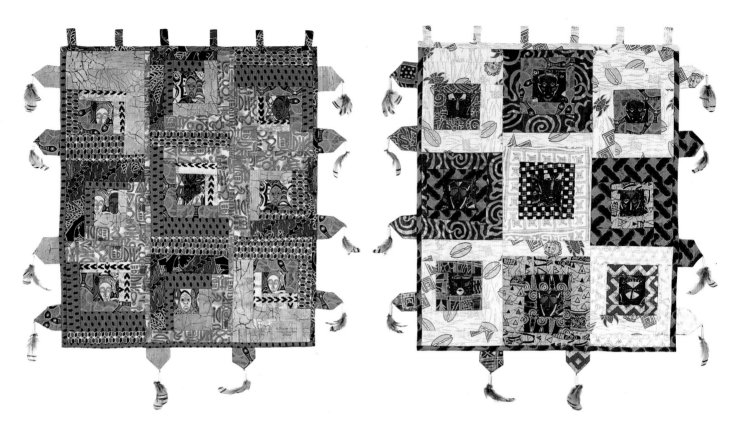

African Jazz

24" x 28"
Mary E. Buxton
Log Cabin block

Mary especially liked designing for two-quilts-in-one: it allowed her to use a total of seventeen different African fabrics and one hand-dyed fabric. She prefers to work entirely improvisationally, but with this method, she planned ahead before beginning the construction process. Instead of making sketches or mock blocks, Mary cut large shapes and pinned them up on the design wall to audition the different fabrics. She says the piece "begged" for embellishments, so she added beads and feathers along three sides.

Mary loves her finished piece and thought the overall weight worked well for a wall hanging. She reminds people that the seam allowances for both sides sit on top of each other, which can make the finished project stiff and inflexible—perfect for wall hangings, place mats, and table runners. When making clothing or a bed quilt, remember to choose a lightweight, drapey foundation material and grade the seam allowances for a more flexible end result.

ACCESSORIES FOR THE HOME

Black Tie Affair/
Christmas at the Cabin

18¼" x 18¼"
Beverly King
Log Cabin block

The title came to Beverly when she finished her table mat. One side seemed formal while the opposite side looked casual. She began the mat in a workshop with me and finished it at home. Beverly used the standard supplies for reversible-foundation piecing, page 8.

Beverly followed the basic technique to reverse-piece the four blocks and four border sections. The black/white/red side was assembled right sides together. The red fabric used to cover the seams on the red/green side became part of the overall design. A single-fabric/double French-fold binding finished the outside edges.

Keeping the colors straight on both sides was a challenge for Beverly, she says. Using mock blocks or a simple sketch really simplifies keeping the two color schemes separate and organized.

Running Hot and Cold

17½" x 31½"
Carol Webb
Repeat block

Using a block designed by Joan Dyer, her sister, Carol simplified it on her computer and created the illusion of complexity with fabric choices, block construction, and block placement. The materials included Marimekko® fabrics from Finland, low loft cotton batting for the foundation material and the typical list of supplies for reversible-foundation piecing, page 8.

Carol followed a variation of the basic technique, which results in more piecing on one side and visible quilting to show on the other side. This clever shortcut makes the table runner look more complicated than it really is. Block assembly began on the plain side, instead of the usual lined side, with the Combination Piece number 1-7, hot-color scheme. Carol flipped to the lined side, cold-color scheme, and began sewing the seven individual pieces together in order, triangle, five rectangles, and triangle. The bobbin thread "quilted" the big piece on the plain

side. The rest of the block was assembled according to the basic technique.

Simple rotations of the eight Repeat blocks create the strong geometric pattern. The contrasting sashing on both sides plays an important role in the overall design. The table runner is completed with a border and single-fabric/double French-fold binding.

Carol recommends trying this variation of the basic technique to minimize the amount of piecing while at the same time adding visible quilting to one side.

CLOTHING AND ACCESSORIES

Two for One Vest

Karen Boutte
Repeat block

Karen's suitcase will be a little lighter on her next trip when she packs her reversible fingertip length vest, one black sweater, and one pair of black pants for two days of outfits. She modified a commercial vest pattern to use with a simple but effective tulip block. With flannel as the foundation material, Karen put together ethnic fabrics along with the typical supplies for reversible-foundation piecing, see page 8.

Karen followed the basic technique with one modification. Instead of piecing and connecting six individual blocks, she cut out the entire vest fronts in flannel. Next she heat transferred the block design exactly where she wanted it, three blocks to each front. After reverse-foundation piecing the block designs, Karen added sashing between the blocks, along the vest sides and shoulder area.

Before assembling the vest pattern, she quilted the vest back pieces with flannel, following the grid on the Japanese fabric. She sewed the vest right sides together, and finished the other side with bias binding. A weighted tie at the neck closes the vest from both sides.

Karen said she loved using the pin-poke method to position the fabrics. She also offered these hints: make a "test" sample block first; view your work from a distance to check for balance, value, and pattern placement; cut out all block pieces at once to avoid running out of fabrics; and buy lots of pins.

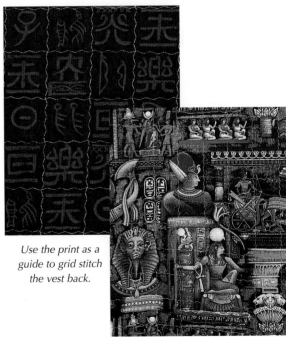

Use the print as a guide to grid stitch the vest back.

Metallic thread accents print

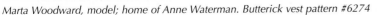
Marta Woodward, model; home of Anne Waterman. Butterick vest pattern #6274

Marta Woodward, model; home of
Sandra Bruce and Gary Pierazzi

Bog Coat

Kathleen George Douglas
Strip-Piecing patterns

Kathleen just happened to be in
the middle of making a series of
bog coats, each one with a unique
group of materials and methods.
When she received the instructions for using reversible-foundation piecing, the idea for this bog
coat came quickly to the surface.
Kathleen hand-stamped silk organza for the foundation material then
assembled her own hand-dyed silk
organza pieces for both sides of
the coat. She marked the sewing
lines with blue pencil. Other
materials included assorted rayon
and metallic threads, and seed beads.

Kathleen was able to follow a
variation of the basic technique
requiring no templates. Her strip-
pieced pattern, with roughly parallel pieces, allowed her to sew each
seam twice to piece both sides.
This shortcut can only be used
with these kinds of block patterns.

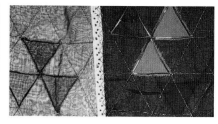

Detail of bog coat

Kathleen reinforced the strip-
pieced organza by topstitching $\frac{1}{4}''$
from each seam and then surface
stitched with an assortment of
thread colors. She took advantage
of the assembly process to add
design elements to her coat. The
three reverse-pieced panels were
assembled with high-contrast,
blue-violet fabric strips, machine
stitched in place. The sleeve seam
on the warm color side is encased
in the same blue-violet fabric and
left to hang free, reminiscent of a
kimono sleeve. The body (lower
half) of the coat is one piece of
blue-violet silk organza stitched
and appliquéd with triangles of
contrasting colors. The single-
fabric/double French-fold binding
was embellished with stitching
and hand-sewn seed beads.

Kathleen is very pleased with her
experiment with sheer fabric,
color, and pattern. Kathleen advises giving the silk organza a good
starching with dissolved Solvey®,
a water-soluble stabilizer by Sulky,
and using lots of pins to hold it all
together while sewing. Sewing
with silk organza can be trying.
Now Kathleen remembers why
she hasn't been doing much piecing
with silk organza lately!

Josie's Coat

Carole Elsbree

Fan blocks

After taking one of my workshops, Carole decided to make her next project reversible. With her commercial jacket pattern and an assortment of fabrics ready to go, she was "forced" to buy more fabric for the reverse side of the jacket. She used muslin for the foundation material to keep the jacket light-weight, about forty-five fabrics altogether, and the usual supplies for reversible-foundation piecing, see page 8. Two antique buttons from her mother-in-law's collection completed the supply list.

Carole transferred the entire block design to muslin. Next, she reverse-pieced the center arc first, following the basic technique. Using a plastic template for the arc shape, she carefully trimmed off the excess fabric leaving a generous $1/4$" seam allowance and the foundation material intact. Finally, she sewed the background and quarter circle pieces to the block, right sides together, both sides at the same time. Carole clipped the seam allowances before ironing. For alternative methods to assemble Fan type blocks, see pages 56, 64, and 65.

To assemble the coat, Carole sewed the blocks into a panel, right sides together, then covered up the seams on the all-blue side with low-contrast teal fabric. She cut out her pattern pieces from the pieced panel and carried on with making the coat, covering up the seams with the same teal fabric. The outside edges were finished with a single-fabric/double French-fold binding. One loop, inserted into the binding, closes the jacket for both sides.

Adapt this idea to your favorite commercial pattern, or make a quilt; both start with a panel of connected blocks. As an alternative, sashing could be used between the blocks (instead of sewing the blocks directly together). Carole advises readers to practice first, be very careful, and go slowly in the beginning. Reverse-piecing New York Beauty type blocks is very challenging, but the effort really paid off for Carole with her beautiful jacket.

Marta Woodward, model; home of Sandra Bruce and Gary Pierazzi. The New Millennium Jacket pattern by Eileen Chapman, Eileens's Design Studio

Marta Woodward, model; home of Gloria and Steven Buckley; LessIsMore #90547, Fabric Collections and Cutting Corners

Less Is More
Wendy Hill
Strip Piecing Patterns

Easy reversible-strip piecing results in a sophisticated looking vest. I chose a commercial vest pattern with no side seams for my vest, an assortment of commercial hand-dyed fabrics, cotton batting and the typical supplies for reversible-foundation piecing, see page 8.

Using a variation of the basic technique with no templates, I started out with a strip of batting wide enough to accommodate the center band of strip piecing, narrow borders and sashing. Beginning with the center band, I reverse-pieced the roughly parallel strips using the no-template method.

Assembly of the strips was very easy and all done by machine. The strips were sewn right sides together, with the seams covered up on the other side with a strip of fabric. The machine stitching top-stitches the fabric strip, while the bobbin thread outline quilts the other side. I cut out my pattern piece from this panel and quickly finished my vest. The shoulder seams were sewn right sides to-gether; the other side was covered with a fabric strip. A two-fabric/double French-fold binding fin-ished the armhole and outside edges.

Remember, when finishing outside or armhole edges with binding instead of the facing or hem called for by the pattern, you must cut off the seam allowance first. To do this, I sew $1/8$" beyond the seam allowance parallel to the edge, then cut off the seam allowance. For example: if the seam allowance is $5/8$", sew $6/8$" around the edge and cut off $5/8$".

Using reversible-strip pieced pat-terns to make quilts and clothing is easy. For a quilt just bind the outside edges and cuddle up with a book and a cup of tea. Clothing is just about as easy: make a panel large enough to cut out the pat-tern pieces; assemble the garment; and bind the edges. In no time, you'll be ready to meet your friends at the corner coffee shop.

Buttons from BumbleBeads, Dede Leupold

Rose Garden/Stained Glass Vest

Wendy Hill
Crazy Quilt block

This is not a project for the timid: it is time consuming, repetitious and involves a lot of hand sewing. But if these things don't scare you, it isn't difficult to make a vest like this. Refer to the Roses/And More Roses Project on page 52 for this block pattern.

The foundation material is non-woven, Sulky Soft 'n Sheer lightweight nylon stabilizer. The stained glass fabrics are commercial hand-dyed cottons, including the black "lead". The rose pieces were cut from one piece of commercial hand-dyed mottled pink fabric. The leaves were cut from one piece of a cotton leaf print. The other materials include the typical supplies for reversible-foundation piecing, see page 8.

*Jean Cacido Vest pattern,
The Sewing Workshop*

To make a vest, look for a pattern with separate front and back pattern pieces. Assemble the vest around the reverse-pieced fronts; use the same nylon stabilizer between the vest back fabrics for extra body and drape.

Cut out the foundation material in one large piece, not in separate blocks. For this vest, I traced the vest pattern onto the nylon foundation material and cut out the pattern pieces 1" larger than the cutting line. Enlarge the 5" Crazy Quilt block pattern on a photocopy machine to have an assortment of seven nearly similar sizes ranging from 5" to $7\frac{1}{8}$". Hand trace the Crazy Quilt block patterns directly onto the vest, about five to six blocks on each front, depending on the pattern size; allowing a few of the blocks to run over the cutting line.

Follow a variation of the basic technique, with more piecing on one side and substituting big pieces on the other side. The rose side uses all twenty-six pieces of the Crazy Quilt block, while the stained glass side combines pieces 1-2, 3-7, 8-14, 16-17, 18-20, 21-23, and 24-26. When piecing the leaves on the rose side, trim the seams only. Let the ends hang into the space between the blocks.

*Marta Woodward, model;
home of Sandra Bruce and
Gary Pierazzi, Jean Cacido Vest pattern,
The Sewing Workshop*

After the piecing is completed, fill in the space between the blocks. Cut and shape the green leaf fabric to fill in the gaps, turning edges under and basting in place. Additional patches of green leaf fabric may be needed to fill in the space completely.

On the stained glass side, baste around the actual outside seam line of the blocks and trim off the excess fabrics. Fill in the spaces with big pieces of the same assortment of hand-dyed fabrics, butting the straight cut edges up against the blocks and each other. Cover the raw edges with $\frac{1}{2}$"-wide bias strips made from black fabric.

Hand-sew all the edges in place on both sides. Cut out the pattern pieces and carry on with the project.

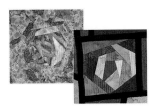

*Detail of Rose block
and stained glass*

Adapted from Vogue #9020

Red side of tote bag

Wendy's Gift

Tote bag
Christine Drumright
Log Cabin block

While making tote bags of all sorts, Christine decided to make a reversible tote bag adapted from a commercial pattern. Constructed from one Log Cabin block, Christine used cotton batting for the foundation material, fusible hair canvas, buckram—for the handles only—cotton and brocade fabrics, one glass button, and one vintage Bakelite™ button. She made the reversible tote bag from start to finish in just one day.

Although Christine doesn't usually follow directions word for word, she said she did follow the basic technique. After reverse-piecing the giant Log Cabin block, she took a deep breath and cut it in half. She assembled the tote bag right sides together and exploited the need to cover up the seams on the other side by making them look like cotton covered cording.

Christine recommends using buckram, hair canvas or batting in the handles to give them "oomph". She emphasizes: "Your tote bag makes a statement with 'perky' handles!"

Find information about reversible-foundation piecing quickly in this chapter. Review the checklist of steps when designing your own project or following a project given in the book. For detailed explanations, refer to the terms listed below in alphabetical order. As you read the other chapters, you'll notice some words or phrases printed in color. This means the terms are listed here for your reference.

BASIC TECHNIQUE CHECKLIST

On Your Marks

1. Choose a foundation-pieced pattern.

2. Decide to assemble block-to-block or with sashing.

3. Make a plan (sketch, mock blocks, full scale drawing).

4. Gather materials.

Get Set

1. Precut fabrics and foundation material.

2. Make the template(s).

3. Make and ink the master block.

4. Prepare the foundation blocks.

5. Organize your sewing area.

Sew!

CONSTRUCT THE BLOCKS

1. Use a template, pin-poke the seam line and pin the fabrics in place on both sides.

2. Use the same template, pin-poke again, and mark the seam line with your favorite marking pen or pencil.

3. Sew through all layers on the marked sewing line.

4. Check placement on both sides.

5. Grade the seams and iron-up after each addition.

6. Repeat until blocks are finished.

Assemble the Blocks

1. Sew the blocks into rows—block-to-block or with sashing.

2. Sew the rows together—row-to-row or with sashing.

3. Cover up exposed seams or finish up the free edge of the sashing.

4. Finish making the project:

complete the garment OR

add optional borders, add optional visible quilting OR

make loops for wall quilts OR

bind the edges with single-fabric or two-fabric/double French-fold binding.

LIST OF TERMS

Asymmetrical versus symmetrical

An asymmetrical pattern is not the same on both sides of an invisible centerline. A symmetrical pattern is identical on both sides of the invisible centerline. The two sides of a reversible-foundation-pieced block are mirror images of each other; asymmetrical blocks will not look identical while symmetrical blocks will be identical twins.

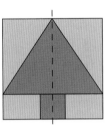

Symmetrical

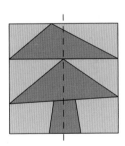

Asymmetrical

Basic technique
See Checklist on this page.

Batting
See Foundation Material, page 82.

Binding
Binding is the strip of fabric used to finish the outside edges of quilted items, such as quilts or garments. Curved edges, such as

armholes or scalloped edges, require true bias binding. Straight edges may be bound with binding cut on the straight of the grain. Instructions follow for the two kinds of binding used in the projects:

Single-fabric/double French-fold binding

1. Prepare enough bias or straight grain 3"-wide strips to go around the edges plus about 12". Overlap strips right sides together, stitch diagonally from notch to notch.

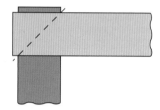

Overlapped seams

Trim excess fabric leaving a $1/4$" seam allowance; iron seams open.

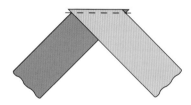

Trimmed seams

2. Fold the long strip in half lengthwise and lightly iron.

3. Leave a 6" tail at the beginning. Use a $3/8$" seam allowance. Pin and sew the binding right sides together with the project, stopping $3/8$" from the first corner. Miter at the corner.

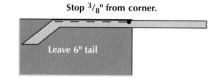

Stop $3/8$" from corner.

Leave 6" tail

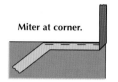

Miter at corner.

Continue sewing from corner to corner in this manner, stopping about 7" from the starting point. Join the ends with a diagonal seam, and finish sewing the binding to the edge.

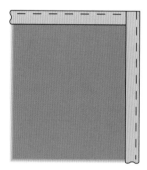

Continue sewing

4. Fold the binding over to the other side and pin. Blindstitch the binding in place, mitering at the corners.

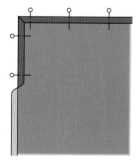

Pin binding

Two-fabric/double French-fold binding

1. Cut one of the fabrics 1" wide and the other $1^{7}/_{8}$" wide. Prepare enough strips to go around the project plus about 12". Sew the 1" strips together and the $1^{7}/_{8}$" strips together as described in Step 1 for Single-Fabric/double French fold binding.

2. Use a $1/4$" seam allowance. Pin and sew the strips right sides together lengthwise. Iron the seam open (essential).

Binding strip sewn together

3. Fold the binding in half lengthwise and lightly iron.

Folded binding strip

4. Position and pin the narrow fabric, right sides together with the project, and sew with a $3/8"$ seam allowance as described in Step 3 for single-fabric/double French fold binding.

Sewing the binding to the quilt

5. Fold the binding over to the other side. The two different fabrics should split right at the seam line, resulting in one fabric on either side of the reversible project. Blindstitch the binding in place.

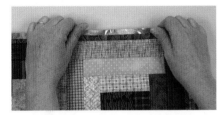

Holding the binding from the lined side

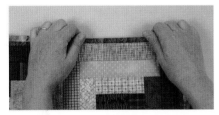

Folding the binding from the lined side

Finishing the binding from the plain side

Blindstitch

This is an invisible stitch used to hand appliqué pieces of fabric to a base. The thread color should match the appliqué fabric. Hide the knot of the thread under the appliqué or catch it in the batting. The needle comes out of the fold of the appliqué, picks up one, two or three threads of the base fabric, then goes back into the fold of the appliqué fabric; repeat to make another stitch, and so on. The distance the needle runs through the fold is equal to the length of the stitch. Try to make the stitch length uniform as you blindstitch.

Block-to-block

This is one method of joining reverse-pieced blocks (see "Sashing", page 86 for the other method). Sew the blocks, right sides together. Iron the seams open. Lightly whipstitch the seams, just catching the top layer of fabric, to keep the seams flat. Cover up the seams with bias strips, straight grain strips, or tubes. Blindstitch the seam coverings in place. Exploit the use of the seam coverings in the overall design, allowing them to blend in or to show off in sharp contrast.

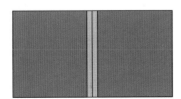

Iron seams open, whipstitch.

Blindstitch seam coverings.

Border

Add optional borders to a reverse-pieced quilt top if desired. Sew one side at a time, or both sides at the same time. The border strips can be pieced together the same way as the binding, see page 80. Remember to add batting to the border strips. Whipstitch the batting to the seam allowance along the edge of the quilt. Optional: hand or machine quilt the added border.

Clapper

See Iron-up, page 83, and Step-by-step ironing, page 87.

Fabric selection

Using your fabric stash or buying more fabric is twice the fun with reversible-foundation piecing. Plan each color scheme independently; this is the magic and fun of making two quilts in one. The foundation material stabilizes the block: use fabric scraps cut off-grain or fabrics other than cotton without fear of distortion.

Finishing edges

See Bindings, Borders, or Loops.

Foundation block

The term used to describe the foundation material after it has been prepared for sewing. To prepare a foundation block:

Woven fabrics: Prewash. Transfer the block pattern to the foundation material by hand tracing or using a heat-activated transfer pen.

Non-woven materials: Most non-woven materials are ready to use. Transfer the block pattern to the foundation material by hand tracing or using a heat-activated transfer pen.

Batting and interfacing

Transfer the block pattern to the interfacing by hand tracing or using a heat-activated transfer pen. If using a transfer pen, fuse the interfacing to the batting and transfer the block pattern in one step.

Batting with scrim

The scrim is a binder, that stabilizes and makes a smooth surface on the batting. The block pattern can be transferred right onto the scrim (without the use of interfacing) with a heat transfer pen.

Foundation material

The foundation material is permanently sandwiched in the reverse-pieced block. It must be able to be ironed; synthetic batting is not suitable. Match the foundation material to the final use of the project. Consider weight, thickness, drape, and loft. The choices include:

Woven fabrics: muslin, flannel, organdy, broadcloth, and so on

Non-woven fabrics: nylon stabilizer, lightweight (non-fusible) interfacing

Batting: cotton, cotton/polyester blend, wool, silk

Foundation-pieced patterns

Any pattern with straight-seam sequences may be foundation pieced. The seams must be straight lines. The pieces are sewn in numerical order, starting with piece number one and ending with the last piece in the sequence. Each new piece must cover up the previous seam(s). Just about any foundation-pieced pattern can be made reversible.

Fusible interfacing

Lightweight, non-woven fusible interfacing is used with batting to prepare the foundation blocks. The interfacing stabilizes the batting and provides a surface for the foundation pieced pattern lines.

Grading seams

There are four layers of fabric right on top of each other in the seams of reverse-pieced blocks. Reduce the bulk by trimming one seam allowance narrower than the other. When possible, grade the seams so light fabrics cover up dark fabrics.

Lined side—trimming seam allowance

Plain side—trimming seam allowance

TIP

Angle the scissors when cutting through both seam allowances; the seams are automatically graded.

Grainline

Fabric has three types of grain line: lengthwise grain—parallel to the selvage, crosswise grain—from selvage to selvage, and true bias—at a 45° angle across the lengthwise and crosswise grain. Foundation piecing allows the use of fabrics cut on any grainline.

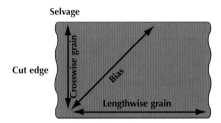

Heat-activated transfer pen

There are many heat-activated pens and pencils on the market. A reliable product is called Iron-On Transfer Pen by Sulky. Use the pen to draw or "ink" the foundation pattern "master block." Place the inked side of the master block down over the foundation material. Use a hot iron to place and press: do not slide and glide the iron. Holding the master block in place, check to see if the ink is transferring. About a dozen copies may be made with one inking. For more details, follow the instructions with the product.

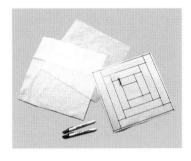

Iron-up

The term used to describe ironing the stitched foundation pieces "up" into place. The clapper holds the heat in the fabric without scorching it.

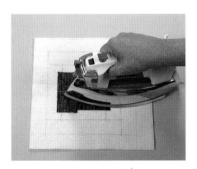

Ironing one side

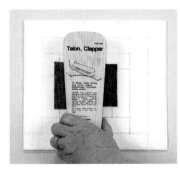

Using the clapper

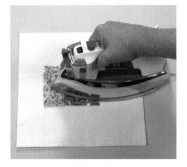

Ironing the other side

Using the clapper

Lined side versus plain side

These terms are used with the "foundation block" in reversible-foundation piecing. The "lined side" of the foundation block literally has the foundation pattern lines marked on it. The "plain side" of the foundation block is blank. After piecing the foundation block, the plain side is the mirror image of the lined side. See photo on next page.

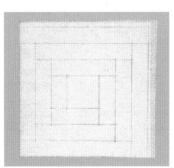

Lined side

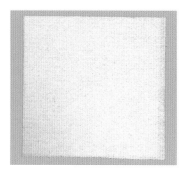

Plain side

Loops

Loops are used to hang wall quilts. Use purchased trims or make fabric loops to match the binding. Use one fabric, seen from both sides or two fabrics for the loops. The loops are attached along the top edge of the quilt in the seam with the binding. Position the loops right sides together with the quilt, placing the binding right sides to the quilt over the loops.

Placing the loops

Make a loop the same way you'd make a tube, turned right side out. Calculate the length of the loop so it will comfortably accommodate the dowel, plus the seam allowance, plus another $1/2$" to go over the binding. For a two-fabric loop, divide the total length in half and add a seam allowance; sew the two fabrics right sides together, iron the seam open (to reduce bulk)

and finish making the loop. Fold in half (seam inside) and whip-stitch the ends together.

TIP

Tape the loop in place to make it lie flatter than with pinning.

Marking foundation-piecing lines
The lines may be hand traced one-by-one, or multiple copies may be made with a heat activated marking pen. See Heat-activated transfer pen, page 83.

Master block
The master block is the "parent" of all copies so it must be very accurate. Draft the master block on graph paper, hand trace an accurate copy, or make an accurate copy on a photocopy machine; see Photocopying, page 85.

TIP

If you want to number your piecing sequence on your master block, remember to write your numbers backwards as they are a mirror image when transferred.

Mock block
This is a sanity saver! Make a sketch of both sides of the foundation-pieced block, then fill in the spaces with fabric snips for both color schemes. The mock block is meant as a reference, not a master-

piece, so don't spend too much time making them. Prop up the mock blocks near the sewing machine for a quick reference while sewing.

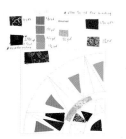

Sixteen Turkish Beauties/ Four Squared Butterflies

Daylight Savings Time: Fall Back/Spring Forward.

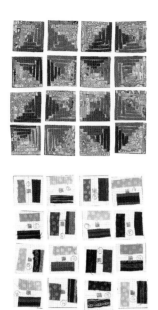

Spyra Gyra.

Several heaps of fabrics

Organize fabrics

This phrase is self-explanatory and will be interpreted by readers according to their different approaches to clutter or neatness. Using two color schemes and two sets of fabrics presents a different sort of challenge, so some kind of organization is recommended, even if it is two or more heaps of fabrics instead of one. Or go whole hog and make neat stacks of fabric in two different piles.

Neat stacks of fabrics

Photocopying

Use photocopying to make the master block or to enlarge or reduce a foundation-piecing pattern. Enlarging and reducing can be done trial-and-error style, or use a conversion wheel to calculate the percent settings on the machine. Always check with your grid ruler to make sure the corners of the copy are at right angles.

Pin-poke method

The pin-poke method is a quick and easy way to "see" the seam lines on the plain side of the block. Always poke the pins straight down through the layers at the two ends of the seam line. Connect the spots where the pins come out of—or go into—the material: this is the invisible seam line. Use pin-poking to position fabric pieces or with a template to draw the seam line.

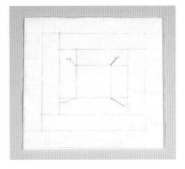

Plain side

See lined side versus plain side, page 63.

Precutting fabric

Always precut fabric for foundation piecing generously large.

Cut specific shapes, adding at least 1" to the measurement. Remember, symmetrical patterns will have mirror-image shapes to take into consideration.

Pre-piecing

Some foundation-pieced patterns use a pre-pieced section of fabric to complete the design. For example, for a house block, the chimney is pre-pieced with the sky, and added as one big shape in the block assembly. Pre-piecing may also be used to join pieces of fabric together to make a "new" panel of fabric. Cut the foundation pattern pieces from this panel and sew them into the block. This is an easy way to add more visual texture to the pieced block. See page 47 and 68 for examples.

Prewashing

If the finished quilted item will take trips through the washer and dryer, prewash your fabrics. Pre-wash the batting only as indicated by the package instructions. Most non-woven fabrics do not need to be prewashed. When prewashing a large assortment of fabrics, each under $1/2$ yard in length, overlap the cut edges of similarly colored fabrics and zigzag together. Now you may wash a large piece of fabric without the fabric getting tangled around the agitator.

Quilting

The blocks are functionally quilted during block assembly since the stitching goes through all the layers. No additional quilting is required to use the reverse-pieced items. Optional visible quilting may be added after the blocks are assembled. Use a walking foot and matching threads for both the bobbin and needle.

Sashing

Sashing is one method for joining reverse-pieced blocks. Refer to Block-to-block for the other method, page 81. Sashing is a band of solid color or print fabric sewn between the blocks. Sometimes a contrasting square of fabric is inserted at the intersections of

the blocks or the entire band may be pre-pieced (such as with stripes or checkerboards). Follow the steps to use sashing to connect reverse-pieced blocks:

1. Position and pin the sashing for both sides right sides together with the block. Sew the seam using the desired seam allowance.

2. Grade the seams. Iron the sash-ing away from the block, first on one side, then on the other.

3. Position and pin one of the sashing strips right sides together with the next block. Sew the seam using the desired seam allowance. Grade the seam. Iron the seam toward the sashing.

4. Add additional batting if neces-sary to the wrong side of the sash-ing strip. Cut batting to finshed size. Whipstitch in place along the seam allowances.

5. Turn under the raw edge of the remaining sashing strip, just barely covering up the seam line, and blindstitch in place.

6. Continue in this manner until the row of blocks is completed. Sew the rows together in the same manner.

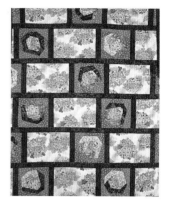

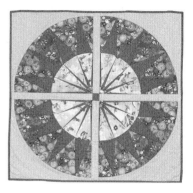

Sketch/drawing

Some kind of a sketch or drawing will save your sanity when making a reversible-foundation-pieced project. If the same block is repeated over and over, one sketch, drawing, or mock block is all you need. For more complicat-ed foundation patterns or color schemes, make a drawing of the entire quilt. Remember, the two sides of the quilt are mirror images of each other; to draw the oppo-site side quickly and easily, hold the drawing up to a light source and trace over the lines. Make photocopies of both sides for use in planning ahead.

Square-up blocks

Finished reverse-pieced blocks will have fabric pieces extending irregularly over the edge of the foundation material. The blocks must be squared-up, adding the seam allowance to the finished size of the block. Here are two ways to do this:

1. Use template plastic to make a copy of the block pattern with the added seam allowance. Place the plastic over the block, lining up the seam lines with the marked lines, and trim off the excess fabrics—be careful not to cut off the template plastic.

2. Calculate the block size with seam allowance. Position a square grid ruler over the block and cut off the excess fabrics two sides at a time.

Trimming first two sides

Trimming last two sides

TIP

Pin-poke into the four corners of the block where the batting ends. Position the grid ruler so the seam allowance lines up with the pins.

Step-by-step ironing

Ironing at each step is crucial for crisp blocks and flat quilts. The rewards of step-by-step ironing far outweigh the time spent doing it. First, iron the block, then cover the spot with the clapper; the heat is held in the fabric without scorching it. Try it: you'll be hooked.

TIP

Use a "tailor's clapper", a smooth sanded wooden block found in the sewing supply section of some fabric stores and catalogs. Or, if you can't find this tool, beg or borrow a scrap of maple, 3" x 10", from a woodworking friend, or you might be able to purchase a scrap from a lumberyard. A plain piece of wood has no handles or finger slots but creases and flattens seams just fine.

Symmetrical

See Asymmetrical versus symmetrical, page 79.

Templates

Use template plastic or lightweight cardboard to make the templates needed for reversible-foundation piecing. Transfer the block pattern to the template material with a heat-activated transfer pen. Number and carefully cut the pieces apart.

Tubes

Fabric tubes can be used to cover up the exposed seams when reverse-pieced blocks are sewn directly together. To make a tube, cut a strip of fabric twice the finished width plus seam allowance by the desired length. Sew the strip wrong sides together. Iron the seam open, centering the seam down the middle of the tube. To use, center the tube, seam side down over the block seam, and blindstitch in place.

Finished tube

Variations of the basic technique

Once you start playing around with reversible-foundation piecing, you will discover your own variations on the basic technique. Here are three variations used in the projects:

1. More piecing on one side, substitute a combination piece on the other side:

Use the marked seam lines on the lined side to piece fabrics together on the plain side—as in one-sided foundation piecing. Substitute one big combination piece—as large as all the small pieces on the lined side. Continue the block assembly using the Basic Technique. See pages 63, 64, 66, 67, 68, 72, and 77 for examples of this variation.

Pin-poke and set Piece 1 on the plain side.

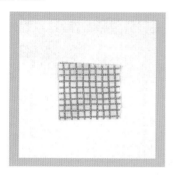

Set up Piece 1 on the lined side.

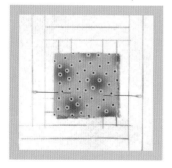

Add Piece 2 to the plain side, using pin-pokes as a guide.

Add Combination Piece 2-3 to the lined side. Use the template to mark the seam line.

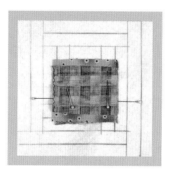

Sew the seam along the marked line.

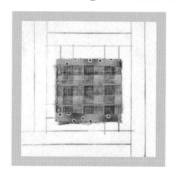

Iron-up Piece 2 on the plain side.

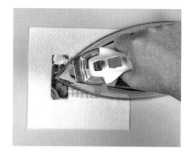

Pin-poke the next seam for the plain side.

Add Piece 3 on the plain side

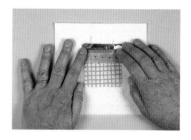

Sew along the marked line.

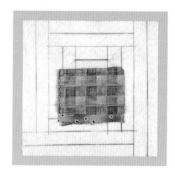

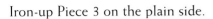

Iron-up Piece 3 on the plain side.

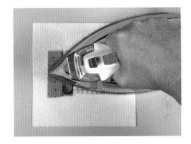

Iron-up Combination Piece 2-3 on the lined side.

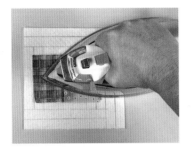

Continue in this manner.

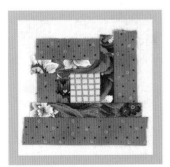

Plain side

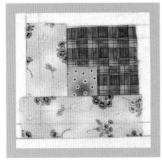

Lined side

2. More piecing on one side, visible quilting on the other side: It is possible to let the bobbin thread show as "quilting" on the substituted combination piece while sewing the smaller pieces together. The smaller pieces are sewn on the lined side, with the big combination piece positioned on the plain side. This is opposite the previous steps. For examples of this variation, see pages 67 and 72. Below are the steps to follow:

Set up Piece 1 on both sides.

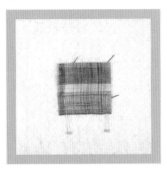

Plain side Piece 1

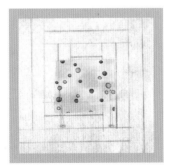

Lined side Piece 1

Start sewing with the first seam: the combination piece is on the plain side; the first small piece is on the lined side.

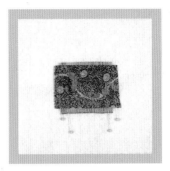

Plain side

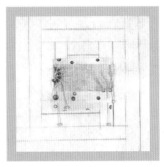

Lined side

Use the template to mark the seam line.

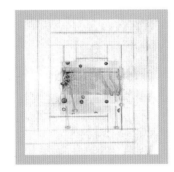

Sew the seam line.

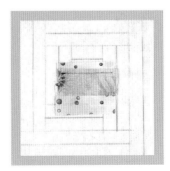

Iron-up both pieces.

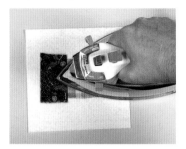

Plain side

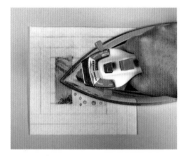

Lined side

Pin-poke the next seam.

Add the next small piece, lined side, and mark the seam line using the template.

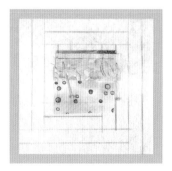

Sew the seam on the marked line.

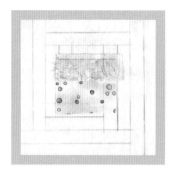

The bobbin thread will "quilt" the big piece on the plain side.

Iron-up the small piece in the lined side.

Continue in this manner to finish the block.

Plain side

Lined side

3. No-template reverse-foundation piecing:

This shortcut is only applicable with strip-pieced patterns, where the pieces are roughly (or exactly) parallel to each other. Each seam must be sewn twice: the first time the marked line is the sewing guide; the second time the stitched line is the guide. For examples using this variation, see pages 56, and 76. Follow the steps below:

Use the marked seam line on the lined side to position Pieces 1 and 2 on the plain side. Sew the seam on the lined side (as in one-sided foundation piecing).

Position Pieces 1 and 2.

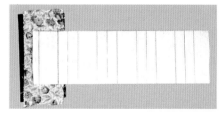

Sew seam.

Position and pin Pieces 1 and 2 on the lined side. Flip over to the plain side and sew right on top of the stitching line.

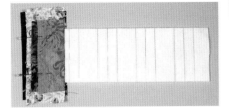

Position Pieces 1 and 2.

Sew seam again.

Grade the seams. Iron-up Piece 2 on the plain side only.

Iron-up.

Pin-poke the marked seam line on the lined side to position and pin Piece 3 to the plain side. Sew the seam on the lined side, just as in one-sided foundation piecing.

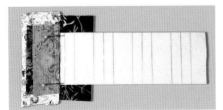

Pin-poke.

Position Piece 3.

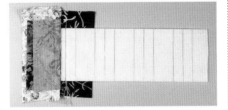

Sew seam.

Iron-up Piece 2 on the lined side. Position and pin Piece 3 on the lined side. Flip over to the plain side and sew right on top of the stitching line.

Iron-up.

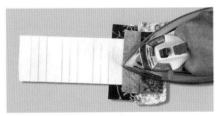

Position Piece 3.

Sew seam.

Grade the seams. Iron-up Piece 3 on the plain side only. Continue in this manner to complete the strip or block.

Iron-up.

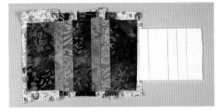

Blue side

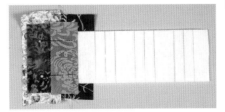

White and blue side

Whipstitch

This is an overcast stitch. It can be used in a refined way for appliquéing, but the term used here refers to a more carefree kind of stitch. The stitches are sewn loosely, through the top layer only, and without regard to appearance: the whipstitch holds down the seams, but never shows in the finished product.

KAREN D. BOUTTE, from Benicia, California, began sewing with her mother as a young child. Even though Karen worked for twenty-eight years in corporate America, she always found time, besides taking care of her family, for herself to sew. Now Karen is very involved with various quilting and needle arts groups.

MARY E. BUXTON, made her first quilt in 1966 but didn't even touch a needle again until the early 1990's when she retired from a corporate career. Now Mary works from her studio in Bend, Oregon, where she squeezes in as many quilting hours as she can. African fabrics are her current passion.

LAURA CLARK, is a craft coordinator and buyer for Ben Franklin Crafts in crafts including scrap-booking, children's crafts, and quilting. Laura loves to travel and share ideas and projects with others.

A workshop with Rachel Kinsey Clark, helped KATHLEEN GEORGE-DOUGLAS make the leap from "boring" to creating things uniquely her own. Kathleen lives near Carson, Nevada, with her husband John, her unfailing guardian angel. Two dogs and three cats "help" her work in her sewing studio while the mountains and desert are a daily source of wonder and inspiration.

CHRISTINE HINDLE DRUMRIGHT, lives in Denver, Colorado with her husband Paul and two cats, Edie and YoYo. She discovered quilting in 1992. Quilting united her love of working with her hands, her appreciation for beautiful fabrics, and her passion for color. Christine describes herself as an intuitive quilter, responding to the design and color of the fabrics she works with. Her fabrics art business is known as "bbgoochi." Check out her website: wwwbbgoochi.com

Combine the thrill of fabric selection with a love for trying new and different things and you'll understand why CAROLE ELSBREE has been an avid quilter the past five years. She describes her method as starting out from a traditional base, then adding her own innovative twist. Carole lives in Sunriver, Oregon with her husband, the dog Abbe, and a beautiful garden.

About thirteen years ago GRACE EVANS took her first quilt class in her hometown of Grass Valley, California and was immediately "hooked." Grace has a talent for taking traditional patterns and interpreting them in her own way, adding her own color insights and design details. A retired public school teacher, it was a "great marriage" to combine quilting and teaching for her church and local stores. Grace has made dozens of quilts, yet still loves to learn something new.

TAWNYA G. ROMIG-FOSTER started quilting thirteen years ago, but she also finds time for working with yarns, beads, stamps, and paper She describes herself as a contemporary quilter who "listens" to the fabric. Tawnya teaches quilting in local quilt shops where she lives in Lakewood, Colorado with her husband Tad, young son Finn, and cat Cheetarah.

KRISTA M. GARRISON who is twelve years old, lives in Sunriver, Oregon with her parents, big brother Matthew, the cutest dog in the world (Annie) and a gecko named Dot. When Krista is not sewing, she likes to catch fish at the nearby Twin Lakes.

Twenty years ago BEVERLY KING began quilting in the little fabric store she owned near Salem, Oregon. Now living in Bend, Beverly enjoys the mountains, streams, sun, and the inspiring quilting community, when she isn't quilting or teaching quilting, of course.

LILA KRAUS, a Sunriver, Oregon resident who was abducted by me in 1996 to make surface stitched jewelry pins, made the mistake of visiting me in the summer of 2000. Not wasting any time, I grabbed Lila's hand, pulled her to the sewing room, and put her to the task of making one-block wall hangings. Lila spent a glorious two days choosing fabrics and making the tiny quilts.

SUE MCMAHAN, from Sunriver, Oregon, has been quilting for nine years. Sue began collecting antique quilts. Inspired by the antique quilts, Sue interprets the traditional patterns in new ways using contemporary fabrics and methods. She teaches quilt workshops locally in the Bend-Sisters area.

KARLA ROGERS, found a wonderful "outlet" for her love of design, color, and textiles in the fiber arts. She began sewing her own clothes at age ten and has had a passion for collecting, as well as making, quilts since the early 1970's. Currently a full-time wife, mother and homemaker, she resides on a small farm in Nevada City, California with her husband, son and numerous members of the animal kingdom.

LARRAINE SCOULER, the Back to Front Quilter from Down Under, lives in the magnificent Blue Mountains, west of Sydney, Australia. Passionate and innovative, she practices what she preaches with two books devoted to her special interests: *Quilting Back to Front*, C &T Publishing and *Back to Front Appliqué*, J.B. Fairfax Press Pty Limited. Larraine dares to be different. Check out her website: http://www.pnc.com.au/~scouler/B2F/.

Coming from a long line of needle and thread folk, CAROL WEBB, of Sunriver, Oregon, was delighted to put aside her dressmaking business and begin quilting in 1987. Quilting offered a perfect venue for Carol's love of color and texture, with the added benefit of no clothing fittings! She uses a computer to develop her designs, and then makes a mess with fabrics to modify and test out the design. Finally she takes to the sewing machine to put everything back in order, including the quilt, her sewing room, and herself!

DEBRA WRUCK, who lives in Grass Valley, California, was introduced to the world of tailoring by family members. Debra was forced to take sewing her senior year in high school. She discovered a love for sewing that has grown ever since. Debra has a new passion for computers and hopes to find a way to combine sewing and computers with an income in the near future.

Please shop at independently owned fabric, sewing and quilt-related shops for good service and good quality products. Look for these products in shops in your hometown, by mail order, or surf the Internet.

BATTING

HOBBS Bonded Fibers

Craft Products Division
P.O. Box 2521
Waco, Texas 76702

Premium cotton, polyester, cotton/polyester blend and washable wool battings made to quilters' specifications. Look for these products at a retailer near you.

Richland Silk Company

P.O. Box 311
Palmyra, Michigan 49268
(517) 263-4756
www.RICHLANDSILK.com

Silk batting, silk thread, silk comforters, silk blankets and silk cosmetics. Order these products directly from the company.

THE CLAPPER

D'Leas Fabric & Button Studio

(303) 388-5665

June Tailor

(800) 844-5400

FABRIC

Hoffman Fabrics International

www.hoffmanfabrics.com

Look for Hoffman fabrics at a retailer near you.

Kat's Clothing

Kathleen Douglas
3001 Brenda Way
Washue Valley, Nevada 89704
(775) 849-8283
ww.katscloth.com
katscloth@worldnet.att.net

Custom dyed fabrics for creating art-to-wear.

Johansen Dyeworks

Linda Johansen
465 SE Bridgeway
Corvalis, Oregon 97333-1233

Hand-dyed color gradations in fat eighths, fat quarters, and one yard pieces. One-of-a-kind pieces, overdyes, Shibori and hand-painted fabric in fat quarters and one yard lengths. Larger hand-dyed pieces for full size Hawaiian Applique. Order these products directly from the company.

P & B Textiles

www.pbtex.com

Look for P&B fabrics at a retailer near you.

PATTERNS

D'Leas Fabric & Button Studio

Private Pattern Collection
2719 E. 3rd Street
Denver, Colorado 80206
(303) 388-5665

(Artist Duster pattern, page 40)

Fabric Collections & Cutting Corners

930 Orange Avenue
Winter Park, Florida 32789
(407) 740-7737
www.fabriccollections.com

(EastMeetsWest 13046, page 51 and LessIsMore 90547, page 76)

The Sewing Workshop

2010 Balboa Street
San Francisco, California 94121
(415) 221-SEWS
FAX: (415) 221-4467

(Jean Cacicedo Vest, page 77)

SUPPLIES

Bumblebeads

Dede Leupold
Polymer Clay Beads & Buttons
P.O. Box 9342
Bend, Oregon 97708

Ask for color brochure. Dede combines the millefiori of the glass bead maker and the pattern piecework of the quiltmaker in her work. She concentrates on detail in miniature designs. Custom work considered.

Schmetz Needles

Look for this product at your local quilt or fabric store.

Sulky of America

Speedstitch
3113 Broadpoint Drive
Harbor Heights, Florida 33983
(800) 874-4115
www.sulky.com

Assorted products, including rayon thread, Iron-On Transfer Pens, Soft 'n Sheer nylon stabilizer, Solvey and Super Solvey (water soluble stabilizer), books, and so on, can be purchased directly from Speedstitch or the website, or look for these products at a retailer near you.

FABRIC AND SUPPLIES

Cotton Patch Mail Order
3405 Brown Avenue, Dept. CTB
Lafayette, CA 94549
E-mail: quiltusa@yahoo.com
http://www.quiltusa.com
(800) 835-4418
(925) 283-7883

I grew up sewing and drawing and making things with both my father and my mother.

When I was five years old, my mother and I made a bow tie quilt for my doll. Before I made my next quilt at age 19, I made doll clothes and then clothing for myself. When people say "You must have so much patience", I think patience is easy when you thoroughly enjoy what you are doing.

When asked for advice, I say:

Getting started: Choose a project within your sewing ability and time restraints, and then trust your own experience and common sense to see you through to the end of the project. Rules: use your own experience and knowledge of cause and effect to make your own rules as you create each project.

Using color: Some people seem to be born with an intuitive feel for using color. The rest of us must practice. Read books. Imitate the color combinations found in nature. Collect color combinations found in catalogs. If you want to use color in a new way, do the opposite of what "feels" right. Until you gain your own confidence, avoid following advice from well-meaning friends.

On life: Never ever allow the cat to bring in live rodents while you are trying to sew. Since you can't control all of the distractions that life offers, SCHEDULE your sewing time along with other activities of daily living.

Another book by Wendy Hill

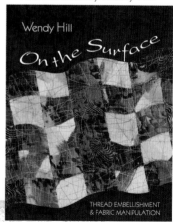

Wendy Hill

On the Surface

THREAD EMBELLISHMENT
& FABRIC MANIPULATION

Index

250 Continuous-Line Quilting Designs for Hand, Machine & Long-Arm Quilters, Laura Lee Fritz

An Amish Adventure: 2nd Edition, Roberta Horton

Anatomy of a Doll: The Fabric Sculptor's Handbook, Susanna Oroyan

The Art of Machine Piecing: Quality Workmanship Through a Colorful Journey, Sally Collins

The Art of Classic Quiltmaking, Harriet Hargrave and Sharyn Craig

Block Magic: Over 50 Fun & Easy Blocks made from Squares and Rectangles, Nancy Johnson-Srebro

Color From the Heart: Seven Great Ways to Make Quilts with Colors You Love, Gai Perry

Color Play: Easy Steps to Imaginative Color in Quilts, Joen Wolfrom

Cotton Candy Quilts: Using Feedsacks, Vintage and Reproduction Fabrics, Mary Mashuta

Cut-Loose Quilts: Stack, Slice, Switch & Sew, Jan Mullen

Diane Phalen Quilts: 10 Projects to Celebrate the Seasons, Diane Phalen

Fabric Shopping with Alex Anderson, Seven Projects to Help You: Make, Successful Choices, Build Your Confidence, Add to Your Fabric Stash, Alex Anderson

Fantastic Fabric Folding: Innovative Quilting Projects, Rebecca Wat

Flower Pounding: Quilt Projects for All Ages, Amy Sandrin & Ann Frischkorn

Freddy's House: Brilliant Color in Quilts, Freddy Moran

Free Stuff for Doll Lovers on the Internet, Judy Heim and Gloria Hansen

Free Stuff for Gardeners on the Internet, Judy Heim and Gloria Hansen

Free Stuff for Quilters on the Internet, 3rd Ed. Judy Heim and Gloria Hansen

Free Stuff for Traveling Quilters on the Internet, Gloria Hansen

Ghost Layers & Color Washes: Three Steps to Spectacular Quilts, Katie Pasquini Masopust

Great Lakes, Great Quilts: 12 Projects Celebrating Quilting Traditions, Marsha McDowel

Hand Appliqué with Alex Anderson: Seven Projects for Hand Appliqué, Alex Anderson

Hand Quilting with Alex Anderson: Six Projects for Hand Quilters, Alex Anderson

In the Nursery: Creative Quilts and Designer Touches, Jennifer Sampou & Carolyn Schmitz

Laurel Burch Quilts: Kindred Creatures, Laurel Burch

Lone Star Quilts and Beyond: Projects and Inspiration, Jan Krentz

Magical Four-Patch and Nine-Patch Quilts, Yvonne Porcella

Make Any Block Any Size, Joen Wolfrom

On the Surface: Thread Embellishment & Fabric Manipulation, Wendy Hill

Pieced Flowers, Ruth B. McDowell

Piecing: Expanding the Basics, Ruth B. McDowell

Quilted Memories: Celebrations of Life, Mary Lou Weidman

Quilting Back to Front: Fun & Easy No-Mark Techniques, Larraine Scouler

Quilting with Carol Armstrong: 30 Quilting Patterns, Appliqué Designs, 16 Projects, Carol Armstrong

Quilts for Guys: 15 Fun Projects For Your Favorite Fella

Quilts, Quilts, and More Quilts! Diana McClun and Laura Nownes

Say It with Quilts, Diana McClun and Laura Nownes

Smashing Sets: Exciting Ways to Arrange Quilt Blocks, Margaret J. Miller

Snowflakes & Quilts, Paula Nadelstern

Start Quilting with Alex Anderson, 2nd Edition: Six Projects for First-Time Quilters, Alex Anderson

Strips 'n Curves: A New Spin on Strip Piecing, Louisa Smith

Travels with Peaky and Spike: Doreen Speckmann's Quilting Adventures, Doreen Speckmann

For more information write for a free catalog:

C&T Publishing, Inc.
P.O. Box 1456
Lafayette, CA 94549
(800) 284-1114
e-mail: ctinfo@ctpub.com
website: www.ctpub.com